CONTEMPORARY LAW SERIES

HARRY H. WELLINGTON

Interpreting the

Constitution

THE SUPREME COURT

AND THE PROCESS OF

ADJUDICATION

Yale University Press   New Haven & London

Designed by Richard Hendel.
Set in Sabon type by
Eastern Typesetting Co., South Windsor, Connecticut.
Printed in the United States of America by
Vail-Ballou Press, Binghamton, New York.

Library of Congress Cataloging-in-Publication Data
Wellington, Harry H.
    Interpreting the Constitution: the Supreme Court and the
    process of adjudication / Harry H. Wellington.
            p.   cm.—(Contemporary law series)
    Includes bibliographical references and index.
    ISBN 0-300-04881-5 (cloth)
            0-300-05672-9 (pbk.)
    1. Judicial review—United States.   2. United States—
    Constitutional law—Interpretation and construction.   3. Judicial
    process—United States.   I. Title.   II. Series.
    KF4575.W45   1991
    342.73′02—dc20
    [347.3022]   90-44755

A catalogue record for this book is available from the British
Library.

The paper in this book meets the guidelines for permanence and
durability of the Committee on Production Guidelines for Book
Longevity of the Council on Library Resources.

10   9   8   7   6   5   4   3   2

To the memory of three Yale Law School colleagues:
Alexander M. Bickel, Robert M. Cover, and Arthur A. Leff.
Each died young. Each, through his writing and teaching,
has made a distinctive contribution to the shape of
contemporary legal thought.

CONTENTS

This short book is the first in a series to be published by Yale University Press on a variety of legal subjects. The series aims to make available to the nonexpert—whether student, lawyer, or layperson—some prominent and controversial subjects engaging contemporary legal thought.

While the law is central to many aspects of American life, few who have not been to professional school have had an opportunity to study it, and most who have had professional legal training have become specialists, able only vaguely to remember other areas of their calling. It is my hope that this book and those that follow will mitigate, if not remedy, this condition.

The series will not be comprehensive. Its ambition is to explore some controversial subjects in ways that may themselves be controversial. The author of each book in the series will have a point of view and will not be reluctant to express it.

I have tried to do just that, and if I have been persuasive my book should be of interest to students of the Supreme Court—academics and journalists—as well as to its primary audience.

I have tried to write with as little jargon as my skills permit. This book is not a reference work and so I have indulged a liberty: there is a minimum of specific documentation. No law review would be happy with the paucity of footnotes found in these few pages.

The book grew out of a seminar I offered at Yale Law School. I am indebted to the many students there who taught me to see ancient problems from a youthful viewpoint (not that this book is in any way a direct translation of that viewpoint).

I am especially grateful to Lawrence Douglas, Michael O'Neill, and Michael Townsend, who continued the seminar as my research assistants, and to Jody Kraus and Andrew Koppelman, who also did research for me. My thanks too to Amy L. Katz and John Wellington, each of whom read the book in manuscript and made helpful suggestions. I also want to thank my secretary, Isabel Poludnewycz, and my editors at Yale University Press, John Covell and Fred Kameny. All three did their work in ways that showed them to be masters of their respective professions. Finally, my thanks go to Dean Guido Calabresi, who provided environmental support, and to Sheila Wellington, who as secretary of the University gave me a house and as my wife the love that made it into a home.

Some parts of some chapters have appeared in different form in professional journals. But over the years I have changed my mind more than a little. Accordingly, everything has been rethought as well as re-presented in a format that I believe is appropriate for the Contemporary Law Series and the readers we hope it will attract.

The fundamental law governing the United States of America is the Constitution. It is very short. Even with its amendments it has been reproduced in these pages as a slim appendix.

Good constitutions are usually short. Yet they are meant to order the future for unborn generations. Ours is a good constitution and it has endured.

Why? How can a document the bulk of which was drafted more than two hundred years ago retain its central place in our atlas of national values? How can it delineate the structure of government and the basic rights of individuals in today's complex society?

This book, if it is successful, will help in the search for answers to these questions. I maintain that some of the answers can be traced to the courts, especially the Supreme Court, and to the process of adjudication. One thing about the process is clear: it is heavily concerned with the interpretation of our good, but surely not perfect, Constitution.

This book addresses some aspects of that interpretive enterprise. Specifically it asks and examines how public values function in the elaboration of constitutional provisions, especially the due process clause of the Fourteenth Amendment. This means that substantively the book is concerned with constitutional privacy, especially abortion.

But on another level the book is mainly about the process of adjudication and the place of the Supreme Court in interpreting the Constitution. In chapter 1 I give attention to two aspects of adjudication: regulation and the resolution of disputes. One difficult question that emerges is how we in a democracy can tolerate regulation without representation. I believe that this is a problem for all adjudication, common-law and statutory as well as constitutional. It is true, however, that special problems are raised by adjudication involving the constitutionality of legislation—or, as it is called, judicial review. In chapter 2 I examine these problems and try to justify the practice.

To justify judicial review is not necessarily to accept the modalities of its exercise—that is, the approaches to constitutional interpretation taken by the Court and others. In chapters 3 and 4 I inspect certain modalities that I describe as flawed, including the politically popular doctrine of "original intent."

I then describe an approved style of constitutional interpretation: the common-law method, which I discuss in the context of the judicial process. In examining how this process influences interpretation I espouse some commonsense, although academically disputed, notions: that interpreting the Constitution is different from directing *Hamlet* or writing a novel, that being a judge is different from being a critic.

In chapter 6 I apply the common-law method to abortion.

The constitutional regulation of abortion leads me to worry about the public acceptance of the Court's decisions, and in the last part of the book I explore what I have called the politics of the indigestible.

I acknowledge in chapter 7 that the Court makes mistakes, and in chapter 8 I assert what the Court at times seems to deny: not only do other institutions, groups, and individuals interpret the Constitution, but sometimes they have an obligation to contest both the Court's readings and its authoritativeness. While this obligation is being discharged, we have noisy dialogue. I see this as necessary. The consequence of dialogue helps fit the regulation that results from adjudication into the democratic ideology that we profess as a nation.

PART I

Constitutional Adjudication

CHAPTER ONE

Regulation and Dispute Resolution

Constitutional interpretation in the Supreme Court of the United States is a method of governing through appellate adjudication.

All appellate courts, including the Supreme Court, perform a dual function: they resolve disputes and they regulate the future. A court's decision purports to justify the result in the controversy before it and to guide the behavior of others—whether private individuals, corporate officers, or public officials—who someday may wish to avoid similar controversy.

There is tension between the two functions. The perspectives needed for each by a decisionmaker are different. The particular and concrete guide the resolution of disputes; the general and more abstract inform the making of rules. But it would not necessarily be beneficial to separate the functions in terms of substantive outcomes, even if that were possible. Sometimes the perspective needed to resolve the dispute and that needed to regulate the future together provide greater insight into a set of problems than either perspective does alone. Put another way, reasoning from the particular—as is generally done when a dispute is resolved—can be either helpful or distorting in thinking through more abstract problems. Much of this book is devoted to these issues, albeit obliquely.

As an example of the dualism that exists in the system of appellate adjudication we have, consider the case of S. Simcha Goldman.[1] An orthodox Jew and an ordained rabbi, Goldman was a captain in the U.S. Air Force and a psychologist stationed at the mental health clinic at March Air Force Base in Riverside, California. His religious beliefs required him to wear a yarmulke indoors. Air force rules prohibited this: "Headgear will not be worn . . . [w]hile indoors except by armed security police in the performance of their duties."

When Goldman was reprimanded and told that he might be court-martialed, he sued Caspar Weinberger, then the secretary of defense, and others, "claiming that the application of [the Air Force rule] to prevent him from wearing a yarmulke infringed upon his First Amendment freedom to exercise his religious beliefs."

After winning in the trial court but losing in the court of appeals, Goldman succeeded in taking his dispute with the air force to the Supreme Court. There the judgment of the court of appeals was sustained. "[We] hold," said the majority, "that those portions of the [Air Force rules] challenged here reasonably and even handedly regulate dress in the interest of the military's perceived need for uniformity. The First Amendment therefore does not prohibit them from being applied to [Goldman] even though their effect is to restrict the wearing of the headgear required by his religious beliefs."

Goldman v. Weinberger resolved the dispute between one serviceman and the air force. It also regulated the future in at least two ways. First, the Court made clear in its opinion that the armed services may restrict liberty to an extent that other governmental agencies may not (as prior cases had suggested). This is an important guide for Pentagon officials in drafting rules regarding religious practices, and for Congress in enacting legislation that authorizes these rules in the first place. It is also a guide to men and women considering whether to join the air force. They know that regulation of the kind upheld in *Goldman* is valid, and this might be important to their decisions about their future.

The headgear rule was eventually modified by Congress (as discussed below), but as long as it was in effect, *Goldman v. Weinberger* regulated the future in a second way: not only were Jewish servicemen barred from wearing yarmulkes while indoors and on duty, but a Sikh, for example, who was a member of the armed forces could not wear a turban.

If we think about these regulatory functions they may make us a little uneasy, whether they are exercised by the Supreme Court or by any other court. For unlike the parties to a dispute, people who find themselves in analogous situations have not had a role in shaping the law. In this sense they have not had their day in court. No Sikh has had Goldman's opportunity to persuade the justices to embrace the perhaps distinctive Sikh point of view. And yet, a Sikh who decided to disregard the guidance offered by *Goldman v. Weinberger* would find that that decision provided a powerful and independent answer to the claim that the right to wear a turban is protected by the First Amendment. To put the point provocatively, the Sikh would find that violence—being kicked out of the air force—was being practiced in the name of the law. This is precisely why *Goldman* can be said to have regulated the future.

Of course we are all bound by a vast amount of law that we had no role in making—old or settled law, as it were. On the whole we accept this. If we do not like the law we think we must work to change it. This accepting attitude suggests that the problem of nonparticipation posed by the regulatory effect of adjudication exists primarily when courts reach results that expand, restrict, or in some other fashion reshape the law by interpreting prior decisions, statutes, or—as in *Goldman v. Weinberger*—the Constitution.

The law would less often be reshaped in adjudication by the interpretation of prior law if the law employed in resolving the dispute were clear to the public and the explanation given in the judicial opinion kept it clear. But such clarity would require the law to be static. For example, a court could not take changing social circumstances into account in reaching its holding without engaging in interpretation that might entail reshaping the law.

If the law were clear and static, a day in court would be important only in sorting out factual matters: what happened, when, to whom, and so on. The parties would have their day in court before a sanction could be imposed for failure to follow the clear, static law. In such a world new adjudication would not result in new regulation; adjudication would deal purely with the resolution of disputes.

It is obvious that in contemporary America such a steady state of legal affairs is impossible. Nor is there much reason to think that one would be desirable. Steady-state adjudication would shift to the legislatures and administrative agencies the entire task of adapting the legal system to new problems. Some societies in the past generated new problems slowly. But because of the rapid social, economic, and technological change that is so much a feature of the late twentieth century, contemporary America is awash in new problems seeking legal solutions. As they are currently organized, legislatures and agencies could not cope with these problems by themselves. Indeed they are now coping badly with a system in which they share with the courts the brunt of an insistent pressure to reshape the law.

In our system the law is much too complex to be very clear even to specialists, and almost surely must remain so. The law must also change over time. One way that it changes is through this process of adjudication, through what Justice Felix Frankfurter once optimistically called "litigating elucidation." This process can be illustrated by returning to *Goldman v. Weinberger.*

The First Amendment to the U.S. Constitution protects religious liberty and free expression. As to religion it provides that "Congress shall make no law respecting an establishment of religion, or prohibiting the free exercise thereof." Goldman's claim was that the air force, acting under congressional authority, prohibited him from engaging in the free exercise of his religion. The facts seemed to place the case squarely within the purview of the amendment. They did, that is, unless the amendment does not mean what it seems to say or is understood as applying only in an anemic fashion to the armed forces.

It is almost always a mistake in the law to read literally and think that that is the end of the matter (although you can get into a lot of trouble if you see a sign that says "Stop" and keep going). It may be that more often than you imagine there is no such thing as a literal reading. Did the headgear rule prohibit the free exercise of religion—"free exercise" is what the language of the First Amendment seems to protect—or did it just restrict Goldman's practices? And is there a meaningful difference between the two? Should the answer turn on how important wearing a yarmulke is to an orthodox Jew, or on whether the restriction imposed by the air force was reasonable, all things considered? Is it important in formulating the answer to understand the purpose of the headgear rule and its relation to discipline in the military? How about the purpose of the First Amendment itself? And how about prior interpretations of the free exercise clause—earlier efforts to order the future—especially in a military setting? And finally, in the context of adjudication, how much deference should the Court pay to the Pentagon on the question of whether the air force needs its rule to maintain discipline?

In its written opinions the Supreme Court addressed some of these issues. Perhaps because of prior decisions it did not pause on the language of the First Amendment. Nor, the Court tells us, was there any question on the basis of prior decisions that review of military rules "is far more deferential than constitutional review of laws or regulations designed for civilian society." But this deference, which has no grounding in the language of the First Amendment, was taken by the Court to new lengths. Justice William H. Rehnquist wrote for the majority: "[T]o accomplish its mission the military must foster instinctive obedience, unity, commitment, and esprit de corps. . . . The essence of military service 'is the subordination of the desires and interests of the individual to the needs of the service.' " The Court, he said, "must give great deference to the professional judgment of military authorities." On issues such as the dress code, the military knows better than the courts.

The Court's opinion is troublesome. For while the military may know more than the Supreme Court about dress codes, does the Court not know more about the Constitution? And, make no mistake about it, *Goldman v. Weinberger* is a case of constitutional interpretation. Yet it is a case where the Court was mute concerning the promise of religious freedom given pride of place in our Bill of Rights. But that regrettable omission is not the point of this discussion. The point is that the law of the First Amendment as it applied to Captain Goldman's right to wear a yarmulke was not clear when Goldman brought suit. Nor was the law static, as the holding in the case made plain. The law of the First Amendment was shaped, fashioned—some would say created—in the process of adjudication.

There is nothing unique about *Goldman v. Weinberger*. It is hardly an extreme example of the unsettled nature of law that is regularly subjected to litigating elucidation in the federal and state courts of the United States. And the clarification, reshaping, or making of law in adjudication regularly takes place whether the law in question is based only on prior judicial decisions (called common law), on a statute, or, as in *Goldman v. Weinberger*, on the Constitution. This means that people are often regulated by courts formulating new rules without an opportunity to be heard on the content of those rules.

———

People are often regulated by legislatures as well, often without having had an opportunity to be heard. Even as nonparticipation is a problem in adjudication only when the law is being reshaped, so too in the legislature: if the proper procedures have been observed, nonparticipation should not concern us where a statute has already been enacted. Government cannot address issues afresh for each micro-generation. The participation problem requires that the closest attention be paid where there is a proposal to change the law in a way that rearranges the permissible application of sanctions against a person who disobeys the legislative command.

In theory, access to legislators in this situation is available to the alert citizen, the one aware of a pending bill; access to judges is generally not. Moreover, in theory electoral accountability makes legislators into representatives of their constituents (and this means to some extent their agents) in ways that judges are not expected to be, even if the judges are elected (as they are in many states). We require our courts to stand apart, our judges to be disinterested.

Today there is substantial concern with the legislative process because money and interest group politics are believed by many to have corrupted it. The process probably can be repaired, although doing so will require heroic efforts. On the judicial side, however, there is nothing to repair, for nothing is broken: those who are not parties to a litigation are generally not supposed to have a say in the regulation produced by the decision, although sometimes they are permitted or invited to file so called friend-of-court (amicus curiae) briefs.

The question of who is a proper party in litigation is itself complicated and controversial. It is an area of law involving such technical and often critical issues as standing to sue, and the certification of a class of plaintiffs or defendants. Standing may depend among other things on whether a person has sustained sufficient economic injury by the actions of others to seem justified in bringing a law suit. Certification of a class turns on such issues as the legal similarities of otherwise discrete individuals or entities. Liberal rules regarding these matters may sometimes mitigate the problem of participation and regulation, but they do not eliminate it.

This difference between adjudication and legislation—the difference in the theoretical opportunities of affected individuals and groups to be heard—invites us to consider whether anything in the judicial process (in adjudication) might serve as a functional substitute for access to representatives and electoral accountability. There are two types of substitutes, both of which can be illustrated by ringing some changes on *Goldman v. Weinberger*. First, the courts and the lawyers who argue before them are marvelously adept at making nice distinctions between earlier cases and present ones, thus sharply limiting the regulatory consequences of the earlier cases. Suppose that the headgear rule had been applied first to a pilot who was a Sikh wearing a turban. Let us assume that the case had gone to the Supreme Court before Goldman's and that the air force rule as applied to the pilot had been upheld. Goldman's lawyers might have tried to distinguish a turban from a yarmulke and a mental health worker from a pilot. They might have argued along lines suggested (but ultimately rejected) in the actual litigation by Justice John Paul Stevens, who wrote in his concurring opinion: "Captain Goldman presents an especially attractive case for an exception from the uniform regulations that are applicable to all other Air Force personnel. . . . The yarmulke is a familiar and accepted sight. In addition to its religious significance for the wearer, the yarmulke may evoke the deepest respect and admiration—the symbol of a distinguished tradition and an eloquent rebuke to the ugliness of anti-Semitism. Captain Goldman's military duties are performed in a setting in which a modest departure from the uniform regulation creates almost no danger of impairment of the Air Force's military mission."

Justice Stevens rejected this distinction because it would in effect have preferred the orthodox Jew to the Sikh and represented "a fundamental departure from the true principle of uniformity that supports the [Air Force] rule." But I can easily imagine the persuasive force of such a distinction, and particularly the difference—which was not directly addressed by Justice Stevens—between a pilot and a mental health worker. And it may well be that if an argument based on that difference were carefully elaborated, some of the concurring justices making up the majority in *Goldman* would agree with it. Indeed if the posited case of the Sikh had come to the Court before *Goldman*, and if the Court had stressed that the rule was being specifically applied to a pilot, the result in Goldman's case, decided by the narrowest of margins (5 to 4), might have been different.

The second substitute in adjudication for the access to representatives and electoral accountability that characterize the legislative process is the legislature itself, for the regulatory effect of a judicial opinion is usually subject to legislative revision.

Where a judicial decision is based on the common law or on the interpretation of a statute, subsequent legislation can always change the regulatory effect of the adjudication. After all, a legislature has control over such ordinary law—though it may have to speak clearly. Often a legislature can effect change in the constitutional field: two years after *Goldman v. Weinberger*, for example, Congress passed a law that liberalized the headgear rule.[2] The Court had held that the harsh headgear rule was constitutional, but congressional relaxation of the rule was still permissible. This did not alter constitutional law itself: the Court's interpretation of the free exercise clause of the First Amendment stands.

Frequently the regulatory effect of a constitutional decision cannot be changed by statute. The abortion case of *Roe v. Wade* (1973)[3] is an example: the Court recognized the right to an abortion in spite of a Texas statute making abortion a crime. Unless the Court reverses itself—and it may be on its way to doing so, as we shall see—a new statute attempting to reimpose prior law would fare no better.

In cases where there cannot be direct legislative revision because of the constitutional nature of the decision, the Supreme Court has made it clear that it considers itself freer to overrule an "incorrect" prior decision than it does in a case where there can be legislative revision (that is, a case interpreting a statute). This is among the concerns of abortion rights (pro-choice) groups fearing that *Roe v. Wade* (as modified in 1989 by *Webster v. Reproductive Health Services*)[4] may be thought "incorrect" by the Rehnquist Court.

Is it therefore appropriate to conclude that the absence of access and electoral accountability in adjudication is made up for by the capacity of the courts to overrule prior decisions and to see relevant differences between a prior case and a present one? (Recall the distinction I just tried to draw between a Sikh pilot and a Jewish mental health worker.) To answer this question affirmatively, must we be confident that the ability of judges to distinguish a later case from a prior one is the functional equivalent for the parties in the later case of participation in the prior case? I ask this second question because we cannot generally count on the legislatures: they are too busy to review the judiciary regularly, and sometimes the Constitution precludes their doing so.[5] The revision by Congress of the regulation upheld in *Goldman v. Weinberger* may be thought of as the exception rather than the rule.

To answer this second question, we must get a grip on when it is proper to distinguish prior decisions. We might begin by recognizing a deep attachment to a commonplace ideal: like cases should be treated alike. This ideal may be at the heart of our commitment to the rule of law. It certainly is important to any conception we have of formal justice. Yet we expect departures by the legislature from this ideal, or at least we accept them. Like cases are frequently not treated alike. For example, transition rules in tax reform statutes (designed to make it financially easier for a taxpayer to adjust to the new law) treat one regulated group differently from another on the basis of which group has had timely access to important congressmen, not on the basis of relevant differences among the groups. And we commonly give preference through subsidies to one group of citizens over another because its representatives skillfully advocated its cause.

Adjudication, however, is another matter. Our tolerance for departure from the ideal of treating like cases alike is substantially less. One reason may be that judges, unlike legislators, are not easily reached—if they are behaving properly. Another reason is the very fact that judges are not electorally accountable in the same way that legislators are. This is true as a general proposition even where judges are elected. (The fate of Chief Justice Rose Bird in California is unusual: she was voted out of office in 1986 primarily because of her liberal approach in criminal cases.) It seems reasonable to accept greater deviation from the ideal of like treatment where it is appropriate for voters to punish the offending official at the ballot box and hope for redress from a new official.

Finally—and this is a different sort of explanation—the strong ideal in adjudication of treating like cases alike supports the dual purposes of adjudication. We often need regulatory stability for planning, and this is promoted by the knowledge of the planner that the courts can be relied on to try to fulfill the ideal. In resolving disputes treating like cases alike is an ideal that helps to satisfy our conception of fairness and the powerful importance of equal treatment in that conception. Justice Stevens, for example, believed that the headgear rule was constitutional as applied to Goldman at least in part because he thought it would be constitutional if applied to a Sikh in a turban. And he thought this because he believed a Sikh in a turban would be seen by other service personnel as controversial and would present the air force with disciplinary problems. That Goldman had to suffer to protect another's "negative" interest in equal treatment suggests how strong the ideal is. It also suggests that reasonable people may well disagree in particular situations about whether one case is like another. Indeed such disagreement is often a prominent feature of the dissenting opinion, and, more important, makes it difficult to specify what we mean when we insist that courts treat like cases alike.

If we were able to get a firm grip on what it means to treat like cases alike, it would both improve the resolution of disputes and diminish any anxiety over the authority of the courts to regulate—at least this would happen in a society such as ours, where there is a well-developed corpus of decisional law. We would have a system of law capable of adapting predictably to changing circumstances. Put another way, if we had that firm grip we could say that even if the law were not clear and static it was predictable in application, or at least reasonably predictable.

According to an optimistic view of America's legal system this is what we have. While I am not pessimistic I lack that degree of optimism, in part because I know that no one can be very clear about what it means to treat like cases alike. And given the number of potentially relevant factors in even a simple case like *Goldman*, I also know that clarity is not in the cards. Should this then make me pessimistic?

The answer is emphatically no. First, I take comfort in the existence of that strong commitment to the ideal of treating like cases alike. Second, judges strive to achieve that ideal. And third, they are reasonably successful in their efforts because of the nature of the judicial process, some aspects of which it seems profitable to explore.

Consider first the adversarial nature of the judicial process. To advance their desired interpretation of the regulations that empower or constrain them, individuals and groups hire lawyers. Part of the lawyers' task is to distinguish prior cases that may be seen as contrary to their clients' desired interpretation, and as I have already observed they are adept at this. The lawyers for the other side of course emphasize the similarity of the present controversy to the prior ones. Lawyers on both sides are hedged about in their adversarial roles by the conventions of the legal profession: each argues, as law school professors sometime exhort their students to do, "like a lawyer." And this means that each is talking to the other. Rarely does it seem to one side that the other is coming totally from left field. This shared sense of what is relevant in a situation sharply reduces the number of considerations that might otherwise be thought germane and makes it much more than merely idealistic to talk about treating like cases alike.

The conventions of the profession—how a lawyer knows what counts as a good argument—are a product of many factors, including what is learned in law schools (approaches and substance, social science, humanistic theory, and "hard" law), at law firms, and in the practice generally. Nor are these conventions static: they are constantly being revised under the insistent pressure of social, economic, political, and technological change. To argue in a lawyerly fashion today is not to argue the way a lawyer would have done fifty years ago, although both the lawyer of today and the lawyer of fifty years ago would if competent fit comfortably within what some might call an interpretive community.[6] The community consists of the advocates, who undertake through the interpretation of legal materials (texts) to advance their client's cause; the judges, who pick and choose among arguments and engage in disinterested interpretation (disinterested at least in the sense that it is not oriented toward one's client); and the teachers and critics, who evaluate outcomes and seek to shape tomorrow's results.

Consider second that while the judge at the trial level generally sits alone, if the case goes on to an appellate court several judges will address the lawyers' arguments on the meaning of the relevant law. This is useful. Disinterested discussion helps to clarify distinctions and similarities that may have been blurred by lawyers wanting to win.

But the desirability of a decision agreed to by a majority of judges exposes a difficulty: disinterested decisionmakers themselves may disagree on what is alike and what is unlike. This means that negotiation among the judges of an appellate court seems inevitable. Some thoughtful students of the law however contend that there is a right answer to every question a judge must decide.[7] If this were so and if, as John Milton wrote in 1644, "who ever knew Truth put to the worse in a free and open encounter [with Falsehood],"[8] then negotiation should advance the quest for truth. But the contention that there is always a "right answer" is a strained version of appellate practice in America. For while each judge may have a preferred interpretation, often that judge has an acceptable second-best position as well. Experience at least seems to suggest that this is so. Much scholarly writing and good investigative reporting has been devoted to great cases in the Supreme Court and the hard bargaining that takes place among the justices.[9] This is not surprising: since the Court is regulating the future there is a need for it to express an opinion, and the stakes are high. Conscientious judges may concur or dissent with their colleagues if they do not agree after negotiation. But as a general proposition, negotiation presupposes flexibility, flexibility that is within the conventions of the profession or, again, within the appropriate interpretive community.

The nonpessimistic view of all this is that adjudication has two protections built in for parties who are subject to prior decisional law although they were strangers to the proceeding in which the law was fashioned. These protections, which exist in an uneasy balance and do not function smoothly, may be seen as substitutes for the access to representatives and electoral accountability that characterize the legislative process. The first protection is that where the interpretive conventions of the legal profession determine that precedents are weak, regulation can be changed. The second is that where precedents are strong, because the interpretive conventions of the profession give only narrow leeway for distinguishing prior decisions, disputes will be resolved according to the ideal that like cases should be treated alike.

But trouble remains, and it is part of the reason I am not as optimistic as I should like to be. The "conventions of the profession" may themselves be insufficiently sensitive to the perspectives of some of the many groups that make up the American polity.

Women, who unlike other groups make up a majority of the polity, have had encounters with the law that illuminate this problem of the law's insufficient sensitivity. But these encounters also demonstrate the dynamic nature of law and the ability of adjudication in some situations to respond to new perspectives that are redefining social and political reality. I see this particular story in a relatively optimistic light, although it is far from concluded and there is much to be done. As we shall see, an important part of the story involves the interpretation of the equal protection clause of the Fourteenth Amendment. (Others are federal and state antidiscrimination laws, innovative doctrines of civil liability, and, on the totally pessimistic side, the failure of the Equal Rights Amendment.)

The most famous example of Victorian paternalism toward women in the Supreme Court is the concurring opinion of Justice Joseph P. Bradley in the *Bradwell* case, in which the Court sustained a state law that barred women from practicing law. Bradley had this to say in justification:

Man is, or should be, woman's protector and defender. The natural and proper timidity and delicacy which belongs to the female sex evidently unfits it for many of the occupations of civil life. The constitution of the family organization, which is founded in the divine ordinance, as well as in the nature of things, indicates the domestic sphere as that which properly belongs to the domain and functions of womanhood. The harmony, not to say identity, of interests and views which belong, or should belong, to the family institution is repugnant to the

idea of a woman adopting a distinct and independent career
from that of her husband. . . . [The] paramount destiny and
mission of woman are to fulfil the noble and benign offices of
wife and mother. This is the law of the Creator.[10]

That was 1873.

In *Goesaert v. Cleary* (1948)[11] the Court upheld a state statute
barring any woman who was not the spouse or daughter of a male
tavern owner from obtaining a bartender's license. "Beyond question," the Court said, the state could "forbid all women from working behind a bar." Given this conclusion, the Court found the
classification—spouse or daughter of a male owner—to be a rational
exception to the state's general rule. The premise supporting that
general rule does not necessarily rest on the view of women held by
Justice Bradley in 1873, but some stereotypical picture of female as
a weakling or flower or as something less than a fully autonomous
person is required to sustain "beyond question" a law forbidding
"all women from working behind a bar." Without that picture
would such a law be rational? It would classify all women, because
they are women, as never qualified, no matter how well qualified a
particular woman might be.

Times change, and in the early 1970s the Court struck down
statutes that preferred men to women as administrators of estates,
or that automatically gave a serviceman a dependency allowance
for his spouse but required a servicewoman to prove that her spouse
was a dependent. The argument for sustaining such legislation may
be thought to have rested on assumptions of the following sort: it
may not be pretty, but wives are more likely than husbands to be
dependent, and men are more apt than women to be more experi-
enced in managing money. According to this way of thinking, the
interest in convenient administration of the statutes justified the
legislative classifications, if the test of constitutionality was whether
the classifications were rational. At the time the statutes were passed
it was thought that any classification that could be defended as
rational was constitutionally permissible. But perhaps because the

assumptions could be traced to earlier, discriminatory practices, the Court was moving away from a mere rationality test, though it was moving without saying so. This became clear a few years later. More than rationality was required and administrative convenience would not do. "[P]revious cases establish that classifications by gender must serve important governmental objectives and must be substantially related to achievement of those objectives."[12]

The women's movement was not quite able to marshal the votes needed to pass the Equal Rights Amendment—it needed support from three-quarters of the state legislatures—but its voice was heard in adjudication. To some extent at least, its perspectives became part of the conventions of the profession that argues, decides, and evaluates law for a living.

But unlike women, some groups may not have adequate access to the legal system because they are seen as too deviant or cannot afford lawyers, particularly when free legal services are inadequately supported. This means that the points of view of some parts of society are outside the conventions of the legal profession and are not heard when regulation is produced by adjudication.

Justice Stevens was responding to part of this problem in *Goldman v. Weinberger*: Sikhs in turbans are seen as too deviant. His response was questionable at best, however, for it deprived Goldman of the ability to practice his religion freely. If the Sikh cannot do it, neither can the orthodox Jew.

The legal profession is becoming increasingly open and diverse at the bar, the bench, and the schools. This trend, which has not gone far enough, may improve the situation for Sikhs (and other strangers). Does it not seem logical to infer that my relatively optimistic story about gender discrimination is in part attributable to the increased presence of women in the legal profession?

There is of course a down side, as there always is. A more diverse community is apt to increase the number of perspectives on an issue, to increase the relevance of distinguishing factors in cases, to exacerbate the problem of getting that grip on what is alike in possibly distinguishable cases, and thus to make law more ad hoc. This may solve the problem of lack of access and electoral accountability by reducing the regulatory force of adjudication, but it may be at a substantial cost to efficiency. For if the law is more ad hoc it is harder to use it for planning purposes, or for settling disputes. Moreover, many will worry about the apparent increase in judicial discretion that attends the phenomenon I am describing. They will believe that judges faced with more relevant variables will be less constrained, that theirs is the liberty of choice, that they will choose to make their personal preferences the law. But law made by judges must in the end be politically digestible, and if the judge is disinterested then disciplined discretion in reshaping the law is not an evil. Inefficiency may also be a price worth paying, for professional diversity and the availability of legal services for all are required to justify the regulatory aspects of adjudication. Indeed, the counterpart to these goals on the legislative side is the extension of the franchise.

CHAPTER TWO

Judicial Review

While the regulatory aspects of appellate adjudication in any of its forms may make us uneasy, judicial regulation is generally regarded as most troublesome when the meaning of the Constitution is at stake. This is not simply because constitutional law is often more important than other types of law. It is rather because constitutional adjudication produces regulation that may overturn or veto enacted law, and because this type of judicial regulation is relatively final since it is hard to change.

Consider the standard account of three forms of adjudication: common law, statutory, and constitutional. The common law is made by judges, at least in the sense that the interpretation and application of prior law—so much a part of the process of adjudication—is the interpretation and application of regulation that was itself produced in earlier adjudication. Examples of law that fall at least partly in this category are contracts and torts.

Adjudication involving statutes, such as those regulating security markets or labor unions, implicates other branches of government. These branches are law makers more than the courts are. Here the interpretation and application is predominantly of regulation enacted by a legislature, although prior judicial decisions applying the statute will themselves require interpretation.

Neither common-law nor statutory adjudication generally pits court against legislature; and neither produces regulation that cannot be undone by subsequent legislation. Thus if the majority of a legislature is unhappy about the development of the common law of civil liability (torts), it can change the law by legislation, or at least undertake to do so. Moreover, if one of its statutes is interpreted by the courts in a manner that the legislature takes to be inappropriate, it can revise the statute.

The standard account acknowledges that some observers see in these examples a conflict between court and legislature on the direction law should take and recognizes that some conflict may exist. It recognizes also what I noted in passing in the last chapter: legislatures are too busy and their processes too hedged about to make it realistic to expect systematic legislative oversight of judicial decisionmaking. But the standard account emphasizes that the constraints on courts in the development of law are very different from the constraints that govern the legislative process. I explored some of these differences in the first chapter and shall take up the matter later in the context of constitutional adjudication. These differences tend to defuse conflict. Nor is there any question in a formal sense that the electorally accountable legislature has the final word. Certainly the ideal is not conflict. It is a cooperative relationship between legislature and court, one that reflects the institutional capacities of both in the joint enterprise of ordering the future wisely.

Contrast this with constitutional adjudication, or judicial review. Here one does sometimes find conflict and the potential for judicial finality. The most dramatic situation is one in which Congress has enacted a law, the President has signed it, officials have applied it, and those to whom it has been applied say that all prior governmental action is illegal because it is unconstitutional. In *Goldman v. Weinberger* the Supreme Court of the United States, sitting as an appellate court, had the clear authority to pass on the constitutionality of the governmental action. It had the authority to declare prior governmental action unconstitutional—which in this case it did not exercise.

Marbury v. Madison (1803) is the leading case holding that such authority exists.[1] Marbury, who had been appointed and confirmed as a justice of the peace for the District of Columbia, had not received his judicial commission when the administration of John Adams yielded to that of Thomas Jefferson and his secretary of state, James Madison. Marbury sued Madison in the Supreme Court for delivery of his commission. He claimed that the Supreme Court had "original jurisdiction" to entertain the action under the Judiciary Act, passed by Congress in 1789; that is, jurisdiction as a court of first impression—a trial court—rather than as an appellate court. The Court read the Act as granting it original jurisdiction, but it read the Constitution as denying Congress the authority to make such a grant.

John Marshall wrote for a unanimous Court, and what is most important for our purposes is captured by the language of our greatest chief justice:

> It is, emphatically, the province and duty of the judicial department, to say what the law is. Those who apply the rule to particular cases, must of necessity expound and interpret that rule. If two laws conflict with each other, the court must decide on the operation of each. So, if a law be in opposition to the constitution; if both the law and the constitution apply to a particular case, so that the court must either decide that case, conformable to the law, disregarding the constitution; or conformable to the constitution, disregarding the law; the court must determine which of these conflicting rules governs the case: this is of the very essence of judicial duty. If then, the courts are to regard the constitution, and the constitution is superior to any ordinary act of the legislature, the constitution, and not such ordinary act, must govern the case to which they both apply.

The Constitution did not spell out that the courts were to consider it superior to ordinary law while treating it in the same fashion as ordinary law. Article III establishes the judicial branch and in part provides: "The Judicial Power shall extend to all Cases . . . arising under this Constitution, the Laws of the United States, and Treaties made." And Article VI, the supremacy clause, reads: "This Constitution . . . shall be the supreme Law of the Land; and the Judges in every State shall be bound thereby, any Thing in the Constitution or Laws of any State to the Contrary notwithstanding."

But while this language supported the Chief Justice in his interpretation in *Marbury v. Madison*, it did not require that interpretation. Congress and the President are under an obligation to obey the Constitution. Judicial faithfulness to the separation of powers among the branches of the federal government—an important feature of the Constitution—might well have dictated that the Court respect the understanding that the other branches have of their constitutional authority. This understanding was reflected in the Judiciary Act of 1789 that Marshall and his Court struck down.

But Marshall's view may also be seen as drawing support from the structure of the Constitution and the different functions of the three branches of the central government that result from the separation of powers. Alexander Hamilton addressed structure and function in *The Federalist*, the most famous of the writings explaining and advocating ratification of the 1787 Constitution. He was one of three authors; the others were James Madison and John Jay. Each of the "eighty-five letters to the public" that make up *The Federalist* was signed Publius. Here is some of what Hamilton had to say in No. 78: "The complete independence of the courts of justice is peculiarly essential in a limited Constitution. By a limited Constitution, I understand one which contains certain specified exceptions to the legislative authority; such, for instance, as that it shall pass no bills of attainder, no ex post facto laws, and the like. Limitations of this kind can be preserved in practice no other way than through the medium of courts of justice, whose duty it must be to declare all acts contrary to the manifest tenor of the Constitution void. Without this, all the reservations of particular rights or privileges would amount to nothing."[2]

But in spite of Marshall and Hamilton, the debate has continued. Many scholars, judges, and politicians have participated, and while much of the debate has concerned the scope and modalities of judicial review, some of it has questioned the legitimacy of the practice itself. We shall pick the debate up in the recent past and learn from two scholars.

In 1960 the distinguished constitutional lawyer Charles L. Black, Jr., elaborated in *The People and the Court* on the structural argument supporting judicial review and put a new twist on it. Black wrote: "[T]he prime and most necessary function of the Court has been that of validation, not that of invalidation. What a government of limited powers needs, at the beginning and forever, is some means of satisfying the people that it has taken all steps humanly possible to stay within its powers. That is the condition of its legitimacy, and its legitimacy, in the long run, is the condition of its life. And the Court, through its history, has acted as the legitimator of the government."[3] Moreover, "[t]he power to validate is the power to invalidate. If the Court were deprived, by any means, of its real and practical power to set bounds to governmental action, or even of public confidence that the Court itself regards this as its duty and will discharge it in a proper case, then it must certainly cease to perform its central function of unlocking the energies of government by stamping governmental actions as legitimate."

What a complex system ours is. Because Congress and the President often test the limits of their constitutional power, and—it should be added—because the minority that questions the exercise of that governmental action may be a large part of the total population, our democracy requires a disinterested umpire if it is to enjoy tranquility. Both Hamilton at the beginning and Black a century and three-quarters later insisted that Congress can no more be a fair judge of prohibitions on its power—for example the prohibition of bills of attainder and ex post facto laws, or the First Amendment—than defendants can be fair judges in their own cases. And for the Court to perform the umpire's function, the Constitution must be seen as law and the Court must engage in adjudication. Keep in mind, however, that there are many kinds of umpires and that the Constitution is open-textured: it does not articulate tightly on situations the way the rule book used by baseball umpires does. And remember too that as a general proposition, the primary reason the Supreme Court accepts jurisdiction is to perform its regulatory function. After all, Captain Goldman and Secretary Weinberger had had one trial and one appeal before they arrived at the Supreme Court. A close call at first base is a different matter. Baseball umpires do not regulate the future; they only resolve disputes in today's game.

In 1962 something similar to the differences between baseball and constitutional adjudication troubled Alexander M. Bickel, Black's colleague at Yale and perhaps his generation's best known constitutionalist. In his book *The Least Dangerous Branch*, Bickel was harsh on Marshall. Our greatest chief justice knew "that a statute's repugnancy to the Constitution is in most instances not self-evident; it is, rather, an issue of policy that someone must decide. The problem is who: the courts, the legislature itself, the President, perhaps juries for purposes of criminal trials, or ultimately and finally the people through the electoral process?"[4] Nor were the structural arguments of Hamilton and Black enough. Bickel sought an additional or alternative justification for judicial review. He claimed that the

> point of departure is a truism; perhaps it even rises to the unassailability of a platitude. It is that many actions of government have two aspects: their immediate, necessarily intended, practical effects, and their perhaps unintended or unappreciated bearing on values we hold to have more general and permanent interest. It is a premise we deduce not merely from the fact of a written constitution but from the history of the race, and ultimately as a moral judgment of the good society, that government should serve not only what we conceive from time to time to be our immediate material needs but also certain enduring values. This in part is what is meant by government under law. But such values do not present themselves ready-made. They have a past always, to be sure, but they must be continually derived, enunciated, and seen in relevant application.

And Bickel believed that the Supreme Court was "the institution of our government" best equipped "to be the pronouncer and guardian of such values."

Yet as we move toward the end of the twentieth century, anxiety about judicial review remains. This anxiety is closely related to concern over the ways judicial review is exercised (the modalities), but analytically different from it. The modalities of judicial review are the major concern of this book. Indeed, after this chapter it consists primarily of an inquiry into constitutional interpretation, the sources of law available to decisionmakers (judges and others) as they perform their interpretive functions, and the way process shapes the manner in which they resolve disputes and regulate. The remaining task of this chapter is to clarify the causes for the continuingly stubborn anxiety about the very practice of judicial review itself. But because those causes are related to the stuff of subsequent chapters, the present sketch will be elaborated at various points later on.

The nerve of the problem that generally is thought to create the anxiety was exposed by Bickel: "[N]othing," he wrote, "can alter the essential reality that judicial review is a deviant institution in American democracy."[5] But since access to elected officials is a key aspect of American democracy, this claim slights a feature of adjudication, including judicial review, emphasized in chapter 1; namely, that adjudication contains in its processes the functional equivalent of access. Still, Bickel's contention does rest on two facts; neither one is especially controversial. Nor are the facts really independent; they are in fact closely related.

The first fact is that Supreme Court justices are appointed, not elected, and "hold their offices during good behavior." In our not so short history, none has been removed from office. Put another way, the Court unlike Congress is neither elected nor electorally accountable.

Second, when the Court holds a statute unconstitutional it acts as a countermajoritarian institution. It blocks an outcome achieved by a body that we think of as democratic because its members were chosen by majority rule and reach decision by majority rule.

To get a better perspective on the countermajoritarian practice of judicial review, let's look a little closer at these facts in the context of the American governmental process. My initial purpose is not to justify the practice, but merely to show that many other important governmental practices depart from generally accepted norms of democratic decisionmaking. (This suggests to me that the undemocratic nature of judicial review may not be sufficient to explain the anxiety that surrounds its exercise.) Next, I shall attempt to justify judicial review further and to explain the anxiety that surrounds it.

Consider first majority rule, surely a central feature of democratic decisionmaking. It may seem like a simple concept. Every citizen has one equal vote, and a simple majority wins, in the sense that it gets what it wants. Even if such a system were possible—and there is an elegant body of learning, known as social choice theory, that raises serious questions about it[6]—it is far from clear that in this simple form majority rule is something a people would want to endorse. It is certainly clear that it is not the American way.

Let us remember that while the Supreme Court has announced a constitutional rule of "one person one vote," we live in a country where in the upper house of the federal legislature the half-million or so people who live in Alaska are given a voice equal to that of the twenty-five million or so who live in California, for the Constitution provides that the "Senate of the United States shall be composed of two Senators from each State, elected by the people thereof for six years; and each Senator shall have one vote." Remember too that the Constitution fails to provide for the direct popular election of the President. And it protects the important advantage of wealth in the political process: the First Amendment has been held to forbid significant governmental restraints on people who buy the right to be heard.[7]

Consider now electoral accountability. The Twenty-Second Amendment provides: "No person shall be elected to the office of President more than twice." This means that our Constitution vests the power of the sword in a second-term President who is no more electorally accountable than the Chief Justice of the United States.

If we move from the deep structure of the Constitution to regular and accepted practice within, say, the legislative branches of the federal government, we find further dilution of any simple notion of majority rule or electoral accountability. First, better than 95 percent of the House of Representatives is reelected every two years, and in 1988 the percentage was even higher.[8] It may be that the voters know how their representatives perform and use their knowledge when they vote: if so, the members of the House are surely doing a wonderful job. Second, seniority in both Houses may not count for as much as it once did, but it counts for plenty, and the power of effective committee chairs is substantial. Third, the role— although perhaps not the impact—of the lobbyist is well documented, the influence of the press and the clout exercised by the clients of the legal profession consistently remarked, while congressional staff is ubiquitous, centrally important, and armed with an agenda of its own.[9]

Moreover, the members of the bureaucracy in the independent agencies and the executive branch have substantial job security and often considerable authority over the direction of policy. This is patent with, for example, the chairman of the Board of Governors of the Federal Reserve System, but it is surely true throughout Washington. Anointed though they may be with a mandate from the people, it is hard for the most skillful members of any administration to deal with the numerical weight, civil service protection, and institutional perspectives of the bureaucracy. Policies change at critical times in the life of the nation, sometimes radically, but the direction of these policies is nonetheless influenced by people who are neither elected and subject to subsequent electoral accountability, nor recently appointed by officials who are themselves elected.

Please understand: I am not arguing that this situation is intrinsically good or bad, although in particular cases the results may be awful. The point is not that those organizations able to afford lawyers and lobbyists—large corporations, unions, special interest groups of all sorts—necessarily abuse either the legislative or administrative process, although sometimes they do. The point is simply that they are powerful countermajoritarian forces.

Sometimes it may be desirable for the bureaucracy to deflect the initiatives of the political branches. Elected officials and their political appointees have time perspectives different from those of civil servants. Reelection can powerfully influence a person's point of view—some believe that it alone explains congressional behavior[10]—and short-run political calculations simply are not always in the best interest of the nation. Certainly they are not if the price of reelection is the granting of favors to well-organized groups that are motivated purely by self-interest. But even when the price of reelection is following the will of the majority, the nation is not always well served. A point that Bickel made in justification of judicial review applies to other countermajoritarian institutions as well as to the Supreme Court: "[M]any actions of government have two aspects: their immediate, necessarily intended, practical effects, and their perhaps unintended or unappreciated bearing on values we hold to have more general and permanent interest."

No, the trouble is not so much that the bureaucracy, the special pleaders, and the congressional staffers are countermajoritarian forces; the trouble is that for different reasons each of these participants in the formation of governmental policies must frequently exaggerate the worth of its own position and dismiss others if it is to be effective. These participants are not always motivated by self-interest—though the prospect of subsequent employment has been known to affect present judgment—but they are guilty of having tunnel vision even when they are not so motivated. Nor, on most matters, is the vision of one participant balanced by the vision of others.

One of the justifications for having a federal judiciary, and especially for having the Supreme Court, is that judges as a group are not apt to have tunnel vision. Unlike the bureaucrats, they have the jurisdiction of the generalist. Judges are also unlikely to be short-run political maximizers. Few political actors can be free of self-interest, and Supreme Court justices are a type of political actor.

But Supreme Court justices are far more capable of disinterested perspective—precisely because they are not electorally accountable, or as subject to interest group pressures as elected officials are, or dependent on others, or, as a general proposition, looking to advancement.

What should emerge from these points is a picture of judicial review that is part of the rich fabric of American political life. Majority rule and electoral accountability are very important parts of this life. So are the many other processes and institutions that interact to produce governmental decisions. Judicial review is countermajoritarian; but it is not an oddity on our political landscape. It is a regular feature of that landscape, with structural and functional claims to acceptance as well as textual and historical claims.

The prevalence of nonmajoritarian decisionmaking in America suggests that the anxiety some have about judicial review cannot be fully explained by the fact that it is (as Bickel insisted) a deviant institution in American democracy. And this must be so even for those who believe that any departure from majority rule is suspect because it is inconsistent with pure representative democracy. Perhaps some are anxious because judicial review is often highly visible. But I believe that most are anxious because they believe that judicial review imposes a constitutional constraint on subsequent governmental action. Unlike the decisions of other political actors or bureaucrats, the rulings of Supreme Court justices have the appearance of finality.

If it can be shown, however, that there is often less finality in a constitutional decision than meets the eye, and that judges (unlike bureaucrats) are constrained in the value determinations that they make in constitutional cases by norms applicable generally in adjudication, perhaps those who remain uneasy about judicial review will be able to accept it with more equanimity.

A discussion of finality might profitably begin with an examination of certain types of statutory interpretation, a judicial function that is not technically judicial review. I shall begin with this because I wish to modify the standard account of the judicial function. My claim is that in some situations statutory interpretation forecloses legislative change, that it may have more finality than some imagine, and that it can therefore be more closely related to judicial review than is often supposed.

Statutes sometimes are interpreted by administrative agencies with a zeal that is an example of the tunnel vision I mentioned earlier. Statutes may be read without regard for the surrounding jurisprudence—including its constitutional configurations—into which the statute must fit. Instead of harmonizing the law it administers with the general law, the agency ignores the background entirely. On review, the courts may reinterpret the statute to avoid confronting the constitutional questions presented by the agency's single-minded devotion to its mission.

Consider the National Labor Relations Board (NLRB) back in its springtime. The board had a propensity for reading the Wagner Act of 1935 as if there were no First Amendment to the Constitution. When unions organized, employers were at risk if they spoke in favor of the open shop, as they often did.

Through statutory interpretation the Supreme Court denied the board this power. For the Court to have read the statute as the board did would have raised serious constitutional issues, although the reading might have been constitutional. The Court chose instead to avoid the issue by making an interpretation that was sensitive to the value our law attaches to free expression.[11]

The Court has often been sensitive to free expression when interpreting our labor laws, although it seems to me that there have been some remarkable lapses.[12] It showed sensitivity as recently as in the spring of 1988, when it ruled on a union distributing handbills.[13] Moreover, the Court has restrained the NLRB, seemingly in the teeth of the statute, in cases where the board by exercising its jurisdiction might have trenched on values close to those protected by the religious freedom provisions of the First Amendment. Because the Court did not render a constitutional decision in these cases,

Congress retained formal power to amend the statute and make it conform to the agency's interpretation. But in fact this would not have been easy. It is politically hard to rewrite labor law, and often it is difficult for Congress to be insensitive to values that are of constitutional dimension and that are called to the legislators' attention by the Supreme Court.

Even if the values are not of constitutional dimension—even if they are in the flats, below the foothills of the Constitution—their emphasis by the Court may deter Congress from overturning a decision, even where the decision departs markedly from statutory purpose. *Textile Workers Union v. Darlington Manufacturing Co.* is another example drawn from labor law.[14] In this case the Court thwarted what certainly appeared to be legislative goals in the service of what a majority of the justices took to be an important public value. Among other things the Court held "that so far as the Labor Relations Act is concerned, an employer has the absolute right to terminate his entire business for any reason he pleases" The proposition that had been advanced by the Textile Workers was "that an employer may not go completely out of business without running afoul of the . . . Act if such action is prompted by a desire to avoid unionization." To this the Court replied that the union's position "would represent such a startling innovation that it should not be entertained without the clearest manifestation of legislative intent."

Of course the Act makes it an unfair labor practice for an employer to discharge its employees because they join a union. And of course the union's position was that for an employer to go out of business because its employees joined a union is tantamount to a discharge. This is correct from the employees' point of view, but to the employer going out of business is somewhat different. The employer may find that the cost of staying in a unionized business rather than placing its capital elsewhere is too great, that the best thing to do is to get out, to take the money and run. But the statute is written to protect employees who unionize from being punished by their employer, and to have one's employer go out of business is surely a harsh punishment.

Nor was the question of remedy too troublesome: while reinstatement with back pay is standard in labor disputes, in this case the order of the NLRB was that the employer pay its employees "until they obtain substantially equivalent work . . . ." In short, go out of business if you don't want a union, but pay for breaking the law. It seems that the purpose of the statute supported the union's claim and the board's remedy.

But there is in this case an issue of economic freedom, at least at a symbolic level. The principle is that even a major corporation, generally referred to as an "it," should be free to be or not to be. It is this public value that the Court invoked to deflect the indicated legislative (dare I say majoritarian?) result. And it would not be politically easy after the Court had spoken for Congress to disregard that value and overturn the Court.

Observe that in the context of the case this public value has no constitutional standing: it is indeed in the flats. The constitutional protection afforded business decisions of the type involved in *Darlington*, based on a principle called economic due process, makes it certain that if Congress today made its intent clear the statute would survive judicial review. The foothills of the Constitution would never be reached, let alone the Constitution itself.[15]

In these statutory situations there is more finality than meets the eye but little professional doubt about the appropriateness of the Court's role—however one comes out on the merits of a particular case. Even if the Court did not have the power to declare legislation unconstitutional it would have the power to review administrative actions, and through statutory interpretation it would have the obligation to accommodate particular legislation to the principles and policies, to the public values and morality, that underpin our law.

Let me give a related example, once again from labor law, but not involving an administrative agency. Under the Railway Labor Act, enacted in 1926, the union selected by a majority of employees in a bargaining unit is the exclusive representative of all employees in the unit. The statute is absolutely silent, however, on the question of the union's obligations to the employees it represents. In 1944, ten years before the Court struck down segregation in public schools, the railway brotherhoods discriminated against blacks in the same way that many states did; they did so vigorously, perhaps even with relish. Some employees who suffered sued. Their case made its way through the state judicial system to the Supreme Court, which held that the "fair interpretation of the statutory language is that the organization chosen to represent . . . is to represent all . . . and is to act for and not against those whom it represents." In his opinion for a unanimous Court, Chief Justice Harlan F. Stone reasoned as follows: "It is a principle of general application that the exercise of a granted power to act in behalf of others involves the assumption toward them of a duty to exercise the power in their interest and behalf, and that such a grant of power will not be deemed to dispense with all duty toward those for whom it is exercised unless so expressed."[16]

In short, the common law was a source of law for statutory interpretation. The common-law doctrine that the Chief Justice grafted onto the statute—that an agent must represent a principal fairly—is not a doctrine that a legislature could easily reject by amending the statute over which it theoretically has authority, even under tremendous political pressure from powerful groups.

There is more regulatory finality than we sometimes imagine in the interpretation of statutes, when that interpretation, as in these labor cases, successfully shapes, reflects, and affirms our public values.

When we turn from the interpretation of statutes to judicial review, we find that in some situations there is much less regulatory finality than we generally associate with a constitutional decision. *Goldman v. Weinberger* is an example with which we are familiar, and there are many situations where the Court has held that a state possesses the constitutional power to regulate but where Congress retains the authority to remove state power. There are also situations where the Court may hold that a state lacks power because of federal law. In these cases Congress can change the result by changing its law.

Consider additionally some constitutional doctrines that amount to the Court's saying to other governmental entities: "You may be able to achieve the substantive result you desire, but you must proceed toward your objective in a fashion different from the one you have used." There is a whole family of such procedural or structural doctrines. Some impose considerable obstacles to the goals of the governmental entity under review, but I shall begin with three that may not: the doctrines of delegation, vagueness, and overbreadth.

These doctrines are derived from the Constitution. Under Article I Congress has the power to make laws. How much of this power can it delegate? How clear does a criminal statute have to be to give fair warning to a person as a matter of due process? How narrowly must a statute be drawn by a state where the state regulates political expression that is presumptively protected by the First and Fourteenth Amendments?

These doctrines have been much analyzed; some have been described as techniques for introducing flexibility into constitutional adjudication. I am not interested here in that aspect of these doctrines, or in the notion that by invoking them the Court is initiating a dialogue with another branch of government, as it does in many of its decisions. Nor am I now concerned with an idea related to both of these and to statutory interpretation: that the legislature must assume responsibility by speaking clearly and precisely if it wants to achieve a goal that is either in the foothills of the Constitution or that threatens other public values.[17] My interest is merely with the degree of finality that attends constitutional decisions based on these doctrines.

The delegation doctrine (infrequently employed at the federal level) requires that the legislature spell out in more detail the standards a regulatory agency should apply in effectuating the substantive goal of a statute; the vagueness doctrine requires greater specificity in articulating the goal to be achieved by the legislation under review; and the overbreadth doctrine requires that the substantive goal be stated as narrowly as possible. Cases decided under these rubrics are constitutional; they involve judicial review. Yet they lack substantive finality. A legislature can achieve its substantive purpose, but it must proceed in a different way. Each of these constitutional doctrines calls for a closer fit between the ends the legislature wants to achieve and the means it employs. This idea has application elsewhere. The relation of means to ends is important in the application of the equal protection clause of the Fourteenth Amendment to gender classifications (a topic I touched on in chapter 1) and in equal protection analysis generally. I shall return to this later.

In his dissent in *Fullilove v. Klutznick* (1980), Justice Stevens applied another variety of structural, or procedural (and therefore nonfinal), review. The case concerned the constitutionality of the minority business enterprise, or "set aside," requirement of the Public Works Employment Act of 1977. Absent an administrative waiver, the provision required that at least 10 percent of federal funds allocated to local public works projects be used to procure services or supplies from businesses owned by citizens "who are Negroes, Spanish-speaking, Orientals, Indians, Eskimos, and Aleuts."

By a vote of six to three, the Court upheld the statute from the predictable equal protection challenge that the statute discriminated on the basis of race. Justice Stevens's dissent rested on procedural grounds: "The very fact that Congress for the first time in the Nation's history has created a broad legislative classification for entitlement to benefits based solely on racial characteristics identifies a dramatic difference between this Act and the thousands of statutes that preceded it. This dramatic point of departure is not even mentioned in the statement of purpose of the Act or in the reports of either the House or the Senate Committee that processed the legislation, and was not the subject of any testimony or inquiry in any legislative hearing on the bill that was enacted."[18]

The Justice went on to describe this as a "malfunction of the legislative process" because of the "perfunctory consideration of an unprecedented policy decision of profound constitutional importance to the Nation." He wrote: "Whenever Congress creates a classification that would be subject to strict scrutiny under the Equal Protection Clause of the Fourteenth Amendment if it had been fashioned by a state legislature, it seems to me that judicial review should include a consideration of the procedural character of the decision-making process. A holding that the classification was not adequately preceded by a consideration of less drastic alternatives or adequately explained by a statement of legislative purpose would be far less intrusive than a final determination that the substance of the decision is not "narrowly tailored to the achievement of that goal."

As Justice Stevens noted, his approach raises questions about the separation of powers: by what right does the Court tell an equal branch of government how to go about its business? This question is also present in at least one of the cases of statutory interpretation discussed earlier (*Darlington*), and similar questions are in any event triggered by the doctrines of delegation, vagueness, and overbreadth. For surely whenever a court tells a legislature that it must speak clearly if it is to accomplish the goal it seems to have in mind—and this happens not infrequently—the court is instructing the legislature on its internal procedures. Thus Justice Stevens's approach, his insistence on structuring the law-making process, may be no more than an extension of an established judicial practice.

The Justice's approach invites us to examine other constitutional interventions by the Court into procedural due process and related areas that may have less finality than we generally associate with judicial review. Consider the regulation by the Supreme Court of police behavior through such continuingly controversial decisions as those that established the *Miranda* requirements and the exclusionary rule. In general terms, and without being more precise than is necessary, *Miranda* requires the police to notify potential defendants of their rights; the exclusionary rule bars the introduction at a trial of illegally obtained evidence.[19]

Neither *Miranda* nor the exclusionary rule calls into question any substantive goal of any governmental entity. Both structure the means of achieving an end; both, perhaps, make the achievement of the end more difficult. So do other things we tolerate and even embrace. For example, police unions may interfere with efficient police work and the efficient administration of criminal justice at least as much and with as much finality as *Miranda* and the exclusionary rule do, and police unions are at least as certain to continue to exist.

Of course there is a difference: police unions came about as the result of majoritarian decisionmaking; *Miranda* and the exclusionary rule did not. And let me make clear that I too share the belief that there is some force in the countermajoritarian objection to judicial review. But I have two points to make: first, the prevalence of other countermajoritarian practices makes this objection to judicial review inadequate to explain the level of anxiety that surrounds it—I believe that some of the anxiety springs from perceptions of finality in constitutional adjudication; second, it is time for me to confess that I am not a true believer in pure representative democracy, if this means that all decisions must be reached by majority vote. As I have suggested, I see some good in countermajoritarianism. By the way, and just to keep it all straight, no one who believes strictly in one person one vote, in pure representative democracy, can believe in judicial review,[20] or, for that matter, in the method for selecting U.S. senators.

The discussion of structural or procedural judicial review that I have just concluded highlights the important role of the Supreme Court as an umpire at the margin of the appropriate processes of other governmental entities. It reveals that judicial review, when the Court fills this role, does not preclude substantive legislative goals, and accordingly that much constitutional adjudication closely

resembles common-law and statutory interpretation in terms of substantive finality: all three may make it harder for legislatures to
reach particular goals; usually none prevents the attainment of these
goals.

The examples I have employed of structural or procedural judicial
review were of course meant to be suggestive; plainly they are not
exhaustive. But I do wish to continue the discussion on one topic
mentioned above, that of equal protection. The place to begin is
with an observation made by Justice Robert H. Jackson in *Railway
Express Agency v. New York* (1949). The case involved a New York
City traffic regulation that barred advertising on delivery vehicles
unless the vehicles were "engaged in the usual business of regular
work of the owner and not used merely or mainly for advertising."
Railway Express had violated the regulation and was fined. It
claimed that its due process and, more emphatically, its equal protection rights had been infringed. If safety on the streets is consistent
with some advertising on delivery vehicles, why the exclusion? The
Court was not sympathetic. But in his concurring opinion Justice
Jackson wrote:

> The burden should rest heavily upon one who would persuade
> us to use the due process clause to strike down a substantive
> law or ordinance. . . . Invalidation of a statute or an ordinance
> on due process grounds leaves ungoverned and ungovernable
> conduct which many people find objectionable.
>
> Invocation of the equal protection clause, on the other hand,
> does not disable any governmental body from dealing with the
> subject at hand. It merely means that the prohibition or regu-
> lation must have a broader [or narrower] impact.[21]

Justice Jackson has a point. He is concerned with the relation of
means to ends, with whether the regulated class is proper given the
legislative purpose. But the point has limited application if the issue
is the relative finality of judicial review, as it is for us. For equal
protection cases vary considerably in the breadth and permanence
of the restraints they impose on legislatures. If the statute in *Railway*

Express Agency had been held unconstitutional on equal protection grounds, it would have been easy enough for the state to achieve its purpose with a new statute that extended the ban on advertising to all delivery vehicles. But the situation is very different when the equal protection clause is used to invalidate statutes that discriminate on the basis of race. Fortunately there can be no easy way around such decisions. They are final in any realistic sense because they conceive a nation profoundly different from one in which the Constitution would permit the discrimination to take place.

Yet even the desegregation cases were initially provisional. The finality we see today reflects our acceptance of an equality principle that has its weight in public values derived and articulated as law by the Supreme Court in 1954. The principle forbids government to discriminate affirmatively on the basis of race (with certain important qualifications). Without public acceptance there would be no finality, but at the time of decision acceptance was in doubt. In the most substantive of constitutional cases there is always doubt about finality at the time of decision, because there is always the possibility of judicial mistake and the possibility that the Court's decision will be politically indigestible. When we talk of mistake and the politics of the indigestible (both of which I discuss in subsequent chapters), we come face to face with questions of constitutional interpretation, the modalities of judicial review, and the sources of law.

PART II

Flawed Modalities

CHAPTER THREE

Original Intent

In 1959, before Charles Black and Alexander Bickel wrote the books discussed in chapter 2, Columbia University's eminent constitutionalist Herbert Wechsler had addressed the justification for judicial review and some of the problems with it. The occasion was the Holmes Lecture at the Harvard Law School; Wechsler's speech, "Toward Neutral Principles of Constitutional Law," remains both influential and controversial.

For Wechsler the text of the Constitution authorized judicial review; no structural or functional arguments of the type employed by Hamilton, Black, and Bickel were necessary. But because the Constitution was law, judicial review had to conform to the method of adjudication. For Wechsler this meant that cases must be decided in a principled fashion. He insisted that "the main constituent of the judicial process is precisely that it must be genuinely principled, resting with respect to every step that is involved in reaching judgment on analysis and reasons quite transcending the immediate result that is achieved. To be sure, courts decide, or should decide, only the case they have before them. But must they not decide on grounds of adequate neutrality and generality, tested not only by the instant application but by others that the principles imply? Is it not the very essence of judicial method to insist upon attending to such other cases, preferably those involving an opposing interest, in evaluating any principle avowed?"[1]

In applying these standards, Wechsler gave the Court low grades in a number of cases, including *Brown v. Board of Education*, the school desegregation decision.[2] While his conception of the judicial process has recently provoked considerable criticism,[3] it was his application of that conception to particular cases and his use of the word "neutral" in elaborating his conception that generated extensive and often harsh contemporary judgments from the academic branch of the legal profession. Some of these judgments are telling, but Wechsler's understanding of the judicial process is similar in content to certain aspects of appellate adjudication discussed in chapter 1. It follows that I have found informative his abstract views on judicial review.

What is missing in Wechsler's argument, and in much of the writing of the time (except for research reports on the history of the Fourteenth Amendment and its bearing on public school segregation), is any sustained attention to the sources of law—that is, the sources on which the decision is based. Wechsler emphasizes a constraint on adjudication: principles—the ground for decision—must be neutral and general. But he tells us little about where the principles come from. Assuming that one agrees with Wechsler, he has stipulated a necessary condition for the use of a principle in constitutional adjudication. But it is not a sufficient condition, unless the Court is free to employ any principle that satisfies the constraint he has articulated.

In a lecture at Indiana University in the early 1970s, Robert H. Bork, then a professor at Yale, took up the source-of-law issue.[4] He argued that Wechsler's approach to the application of a principle in the practice of judicial review also had to be employed in deriving the principle. And the derivation had to be from the Constitution. While it is not clear to me what it means to insist that a principle be neutrally derived, it is clear that one of Bork's dominant concerns was with the Constitution as the source of constitutional law and the proper method to use in its interpretation.

The contemporary debate of which Bork's lecture is an early example can be traced to the Supreme Court decision in *Griswold v. Connecticut* (1965),[5] which addressed the validity of a Connecticut statute making it a crime for a married couple to use a contraceptive device. The Court struck down the statute, holding that Connecticut had violated the constitutional "notions of privacy surrounding the

marriage relationship." Later it also invalidated a state statute restricting the sale of contraceptive devices to single persons, and in
Roe v. Wade it used notions of privacy to grant constitutional protection to abortion.[6]

The text of the Constitution does not talk about privacy, and it
might seem strange that the Court would undertake to disassociate
itself so dramatically from the text it was interpreting. It could easily
have spoken of liberty, which does have its place in the language of
the Fifth and Fourteenth amendments.

Probably the reason the Court located the right to privacy at the
center of its holding is that from the early 1900s to the mid-1930s,
the Court had periodically invalidated state and federal social and
economic legislation on the ground that it restricted liberty. In these
decisions the Court had held that liberty was protected from undue
state interference by the Fourteenth Amendment and from undue
federal interference by the Fifth Amendment. These cases are called
"substantive due process" cases, or (because they concern the regulation of business and labor) "economic due process" cases. The
leading example is *Lochner v. New York* (1905),[7] which invalidated
a New York statute prohibiting a work week of more than sixty
hours for bakers. The Court held that the law violated the liberty
of contract between employer and employee protected by the due
process clause; that is, it interfered in an unconstitutional manner
with the ability of bakery employees and their employers to fix for
themselves, without substantive direction from the state, their conditions of employment.

Lochner and subsequent economic due process decisions were
badly received by other branches of government, some of the legal
profession, organized labor, and other groups active in the political
arena. In the mid-1930s the Court repudiated robust judicial review
of economic and social legislation.[8] At the time of *Griswold* the
Court felt the need to distance itself from the rejected economic due
process approach (as indeed it does today).

The Court's reasoning in *Griswold* was as follows: (1) "[S]pecific
guarantees in the Bill of Rights have penumbras, formed by ema-

nations from those guarantees that help give them life and substance." (2) "Various guarantees create zones of privacy. The right
of association contained in the penumbra of the First Amendment
is one. . . . The Third Amendment in its prohibition against the
quartering of soldiers . . . is another. . . . The Fourth Amendment
[which] explicitly affirms the right of the people to be secure in their
persons, houses, papers, and effects against unreasonable searches
and seizures. . . . [and the] Fifth Amendment in its Self-Incrimination
Clause" are still others. (3) According to the Ninth Amendment,
"The enumeration in the Constitution, of certain rights, shall not
be construed to deny or disparage others retained by the people."
(4) "The present case . . . concerns a relationship lying within the
zone of privacy created by [these] several fundamental constitutional
guarantees." And (5) the Connecticut statute sweeps "unnecessarily
broadly . . ." in its regulation of privacy within the marriage
relationship.

In chapter 5 I shall argue that the holding in *Griswold v. Connecticut* is correct. But certainly it is understandable that the character of the Court's opinion—its shotgun approach to the task at
hand and the thinness of a textual basis in the Constitution for a
right to privacy—should have sent Professor Bork and others searching for authoritative sources of law, searching for the proper way
to interpret the Constitution.

This then is the start of the contemporary debate. Before we
examine its content, it is interesting to speculate on what may indirectly have contributed to the texture of that debate. First the
academic side.

Lawyers at universities today are more aware than ever before of
the work of their colleagues on faculties of the arts and sciences.
There is often some lag and sometimes some distortion in the way
the legal academic uses the theories and investigations of other disciplines. But this too has been diminishing, and legal academics
sometimes find themselves—to mix up a metaphor—on the cutting
edge of other people's domain.

Many disciplines—particularly philosophy, literary criticism, politics, and theology—have many theories about interpretation, about the relationship of author, text, and reader. And what could be of greater interest to the lawyer, particularly the lawyer concerned with a text such as the Constitution? I think it is fair to say that exposure to these theories has deepened the law professor's awareness of the complexity and normative implications of reading, of construing a text, of interpreting the Constitution.

The debate involves many other actors, however: practicing lawyers, judges, legislators, concerned individuals, and groups. There are many participants in the debate because of the substantive consequences of constitutional adjudication. To choose the most striking example, what is the origin of the privacy principle that the Court vindicated in *Griswold v. Connecticut* and applied in the abortion cases? Is it a fundamental right, an aspect of constitutionally protected liberty? And how did the justices suddenly "discover" this in the latter part of the twentieth century? And how do we know whether they were right? The answer to these questions has been a matter of no small interest to those seeking to overturn *Roe v. Wade*[9] and to their opponents.

In general terms, what are the sources of law available to participants in constitutional adjudication? What is a good argument? (In chapter 1 I touched on this.) What counts as the justification for a Supreme Court decision interpreting the Constitution? As we shall see, these questions in turn invite consideration of authority: by what right does the Court use a particular interpretive method? And they raise problems concerning control of the judiciary: how are the other branches of government and individuals regulated by the Court to keep the justices in their place?

During the second term of Ronald Reagan (1985–88) all these questions were debated in a remarkably similar vocabulary by politicians, judges, and legal academics. Surprisingly, from all quar-

ters terms like "interpretive review" were set off against "nonin-
terpretive review," or appeals to an unwritten constitution.

This way of speaking, however, is misleading. All the players in
this national pastime are engaged in interpretation. The true question
is how they go about their task of interpreting the Constitution. The
answer—to come back to where we started—is that they search for
authoritative sources of law and should do so.

The text of the Constitution is authoritative. It is also vague,
opentextured, sometimes ambiguous, and generally in desperate
need of elaboration. The search for authoritative sources of law is
therefore the search for interpretive tools.

Some might object to this phraseology. To search for authoritative
sources implies that if you are skillful or lucky you will find something, as in a treasure hunt. And the critics might claim that the
"searcher" creates rather than discovers the treasure. But at this
stage such an objection must be rejected: the problem is to identify
authoritative sources, not to interpret them. The notion of a search
is therefore accurate enough. At the interpretive stage, however—
when the tools are used—the claim that there is an act of creation,
of making rather than finding, must be confronted. Neither "creation" nor "discovery" is an acceptable account: the interpretive
process in adjudication is too complex to be so easily described.

Please do not misunderstand me. There is profound disagreement
over what is authoritative. Some may even deny that the text of the
Constitution always qualifies. But the disagreement is not an interpretive disagreement. To classify it as such would be to turn all
law into interpretation. The disagreement, at the level that interests
me, is one about the nature of American constitutional adjudication.
It is about the judicial process of regulation and resolving disputes.
It is about an institution, not about a text. And this is true even
though one's understanding of the institution, the Court, governs
the way one interprets the text, the Constitution.

Any attempt to understand constitutional adjudication must come
to grips with a familiar problem: how does a people control or check
judges who are not electorally accountable—judges who exercise

the sovereign prerogative of judicial review? In *The Federalist* Hamilton said the judiciary was the least dangerous branch of government. Today the concern of more than a few Americans is to keep it from becoming the most dangerous.

Some politicians, judges, and legal scholars who see themselves engaged in so-called interpretive review believe that when the text of the Constitution is not clear, the question of authority and the question of control are both answered by reading the text in the light of original intent. To get away from misleading usage let's call them originalists, as others have.[10] By original intent they mean that of the framers, or founders, of the Constitution who drafted the original masterpiece in 1787 (some also emphasize the intent of the delegates to the state ratifying conventions), as well as the intent of those who have amended the document under the provisions of Article V. For many originalists no other source is nearly as weighty or significant in justifying a decision. No other source has the same claim to authority. Nor can any other interpretive method keep the judiciary in check.

As a judge on the U.S. Court of Appeals for the District of Columbia Circuit, the influential originalist Robert H. Bork put his position this way: "[I]f we are to have judicial review, and if the Constitution is to be law, so that the judge does not freely impose his or her own values, then the only way to do that is to root that law in the intentions of the founders. There is no other source of legitimacy. There is no other way that we can say at least in extreme cases that the judge has gone off the reservation."[11]

The originalist position (and there are as many versions of it as there are believers in it) is shaky with respect to both authority and control. Consider first authority. While it may be true, as the distinguished constitutional historian Leonard Levy, has written, that "consensus [about the need for a strong national government], rather than compromise, was the most significant feature of the Convention," it is also true that the founders were deeply divided about most matters that were debated during that hot Philadelphia summer of 1787, and that "various compromises . . . occupied most of the time of the delegates."[12] It should not be surprising, therefore, to learn from recēnt historical investigation that the founders were also deeply divided over whether it would be appropriate in the future to interpret the Constitution they were drafting by appealing to the history of their private proceedings in Philadelphia. Nor was there any agreement about the relevance to constitutional interpretation of the historical record produced in the subsequent state conventions.

H. Jefferson Powell, of Duke University, has done the seminal work on the subject. This is his conclusion:

> It is commonly assumed that the "interpretive intention" of the Constitution's framers was that the Constitution would be construed in accordance with what future interpreters could gather of the framers' own purposes, expectations, and intentions. Inquiry shows that assumption to be incorrect. Of the numerous hermeneutical options that were available in the framers' day . . . none corresponds to the modern notion of intentionalism [or, the same thing, originalism]. . . . In defending their claim that the "original understanding at Philadelphia" should control constitutional interpretation, modern intentionalists usually argue that other interpretive strategies undermine or even deny the possibility of objectivity and consistency in constitutional law. Critics of this position typically respond with a battery of practical and theoretical objections to the attempt to construe the nation's fundamental law in accord with historical reconstructions of the purposes of the framers. There may well be grounds to support either of these positions. This debate cannot be resolved, however, and should not be affected, by the claim or assumption that modern intentionalism was the original presupposition of American constitutional discourse. Such a claim is historically mistaken.[13]

Powell's conclusion seriously diminishes a basic attraction that originalism (or, as he calls it, intentionalism) would otherwise have. Since the founders did not themselves intend "that the Constitution would be construed in accordance with what future interpreters could gather of the framers' own purposes, expectations, and intentions," the founders' will, or desire, cannot be claimed today as authority for the use of their recorded intentions. To the extent that originalism is authorized, it must either be because, all things considered, it is superior to any other interpretive strategy (I shall shortly argue against this), or because judges and lawyers after ratification employed original intent as their interpretive tool. Contemporary interpreters moved by that past may also employ original intent, but if they do it is only because they respect a tradition of interpretation. No longer can they see themselves as being under an obligation to obey the commands of the founding fathers. They must come to terms with the realization that no such commands were issued.

Yet the belief that the founders mandated originalism has permitted its advocates to equate the founders' intentions with the text of the Constitution. Intentions become a gloss on that text. This is the most powerful basis for the appeal of originalism. It leads to the belief that the people through their state ratifying conventions consented to original intent as well as to the constitutional text, and that they therefore bound the future to respect original intent even as they bound the future to respect constitutional text (and one to the same extent as the other).

The people's consent is of course the weighty basis for the text's authority. But since the evidence demonstrates that original intent was not meant to be a gloss on the text, there was no consent to it. Accordingly the people cannot be invoked, and this deprives originalism of powerful rhetorical support. It leaves the originalists clinging to tradition and leaves open the question of how much we should count on tradition in the quest for authority.

In assessing the weight that the tradition of originalism should have in constitutional adjudication, contemporary interpreters should know what recent historical investigation also demonstrates. James H. Hutson, of the Library of Congress, writes that "[s]ome . . . newly discovered documents raise questions concerning the reliability of the principal printed sources of information

about the drafting and ratification of the Constitution.... "
Hutson's research shows that apart from Madison's notes, the
standard sources for determining the founders' intentions are
highly unreliable evidence of what took place. It seems that
much of the documentary history was subsequently manufac-
tured for political purposes; and Madison's notes themselves are
radically incomplete.

As Hutson puts it: "If Convention records are not faithful accounts of what was said by the delegates in 1787 and 1788, how
can we know what they intended?" And, he tells us, his reason
for writing "is to issue a caveat about Convention records, to
warn that there are problems with most of them and that some
have been compromised—perhaps fatally—by the editorial interventions of hirelings and partisans." Hutson reasons that "[t]o recover original intent from these records may be an impossible
hermeneutic assignment."[14] But even if it were possible today,
through some form of alchemy, to convert the documentary record into a "faithful account of what was said by the delegates in
1787 and 1788," contemporary interpreters would have to keep
in mind that they do not have eighteenth-century minds and that
the founders were of many minds. What we understand about
them as a group, and about what they thought they were up to
when they drafted and ratified the Constitution, is not only fil-
tered through our late twentieth-century consciousness but is necessarily influenced by what we have learned from many students
who have seen different things at different times in different ways.
There is no escaping that all contemporary interpreters are cap-
tives, in one way or another, of prior interpretations.

Today's originalists would therefore have a serious problem even
if the documentary materials had never been cooked. Their problem
is compounded, badly compounded, by Hutson's discoveries: if he
is right, prior interpreters were not reading "faithful accounts of
what was said by the delegates in 1787 and 1788." They were, at
least some of the time, interpreting fiction.

There are several additional problems with the authority of originalism. Let me sketch a few. Consider first the following statement of Edmund Morgan, one of our most eminent colonial historians:

> For the colonists, as for other Englishmen, property was not merely a possession to be hoarded and admired; it was rather the source of life and liberty. If a man had property, if he had land, he had his own source of food, he could be independent of all other men, including kings and lords. Where property was concentrated in the hands of a king and aristocracy, only the king and the aristocracy would be free, while the rest of the population would be little better than slaves, victims of the external efforts of rulers to exploit subjects. Without property men could be starved into submission. Hence liberty rested on property, and whatever threatened the security of property threatened liberty.[15]

If we assume that Morgan is correct—and this is an assumption worth indulging—and if we assume that the colonists' attitude toward property still had a grip on the attitude of the founding fathers and the amenders who composed and approved the Bill of Rights, although perhaps a somewhat weakened grip, what are we to say about the constitutionality of contemporary governmental regulation that has so substantially reduced the "security of property"?

Once again an example from labor law will suffice. Under the National Labor Relations Act an employer must permit its workers, who are on its property, to solicit for the union during their free time.[16] Surely using the employer's property for union purposes diminishes the value of the property to its owner. Why is this not a violation of the Fifth Amendment, which, among its many virtues, protects property?

The answer may be that today liberty and property are not joined at the hip. They are discrete concepts, although sometimes property still may rightly be thought to support liberty. The constitutional protection afforded liberty—often under the name of privacy—today is substantially greater than the protections afforded property. Once again contraception and abortion are central examples, even after the weakening of *Roe*.

But if at the beginning liberty and property were united, what does this tell us about the fit between originalism and contemporary legal practice? Originalists simply cannot believe that the relation between property and liberty depicted by Professor Morgan is rooted in the environment that produced it; that the environment is strikingly different today; and that this difference permits liberty to stand free of property, to be regarded on its own, and property to be seen therefore as more accessible to government regulation in the furtherance of the public good.

If one were taken with the authority of originalism, perhaps one might try to reconcile practice with belief by suggesting that an extended conversation with the founders about the late twentieth century would bring the founders to a contemporary point of view. But while such an exercise would surely have promise for a public television series, it would be a profoundly silly approach to reading a text or governing a nation. The point is that there is no congruence between originalism and the judicial practice of constitutional interpretation. And while this does not prove in any scientific sense that originalism is wrong, it does not have to; for a scientific test of right and wrong is not very important to understanding the American way of constitutional adjudication.

My attack on originalism has not yet exposed what I believe to be the underlying conception of adjudication held by its proponents. I shall argue against that conception and at the same time against the contention that originalism is the best strategy, all things considered, for constitutional interpretation.

The originalist conception of adjudication would seem to rest on two broad and interrelated sets of ideas. The first comprises beliefs about the certainty of language and the methods of discovering its meaning. The second is made up of beliefs about the allocation of institutional responsibilities between legislative bodies and courts.

An originalist has to be optimistic about the founders' ability to capture precisely in words some complicated ideas, and about the existence of what we know is missing: a definitive historical record to resolve linguistic ambiguity. This optimism has to persist even though the originalist knows full well that the drafting process involves the skillful use of ambiguity and the purposeful manipulation of what becomes documentary history.[17] The optimism of the originalist must also withstand widespread evidence that the meaning of a text such as the Constitution never remains fixed, that indeed at any time texts are rich with meanings, and that competing accounts of the past are attributable to new information and to fresh perspectives articulated by members of the increasingly diverse historical and legal professions.

An originalist is also apt to embrace a strong version of the standard distinction between making law and applying law: law is made by legislative bodies; it is applied by courts. An originalist perceives the difference between making and applying law as a sharp one at its center. And when it is blurred, an originalist will contend that courts should keep clear of any action that constitutes an assumption by judges of the drafters' prerogative—although it is hard to imagine how they could do so, since judges must act.

Nonoriginalists, who also come in many styles, are likely to see the drafting and ratification of the Constitution and its amendments as a process radically different from the writing of a document by a single author. Because there are many styles of nonoriginalist, I shall speak only for myself in what follows, which explains my perhaps too frequent use of the perpendicular "I."

Whatever I may believe about the utility of searching for intention in my effort to understand single-author texts (what did Shakespeare intend when he wrote *Hamlet?*), I start with great skepticism where the text I am interpreting has been written by a committee. For I am impressed that a constitution is the product of negotiation (as indeed most written law is), that negotiation of complex issues usually leaves major problems unresolved, and that language on which people of divergent views can agree must often be open-textured—to say the least. Let's understand one thing: purposeful ambiguity is to legislative drafting what the fastball is to major league baseball. I doubt that it is even coherent to talk about the intention of a class consisting of the framers at Philadelphia and the ratifiers at the state conventions. How do you obtain the sum of their disagreements?

But if I put my doubts to one side and decide to search for such intent, always mindful of Mr. Hutson's caveat, I know that this perhaps incoherent thing I seek will almost surely not reveal itself with sufficient clarity to be the authoritative source of the meaning of the text—even assuming it were ever appropriate for it so to become. Of course, I also know that the Constitution itself is what was ratified, not the founders' intention. Yet I know too that I will be greatly benefited in understanding the Constitution if I learn as much as I can about the period of its creation. For to deny the authority of original intent is not to deny the importance of history.

Nor need I accept the sharp distinction between making law and applying law. Although I concede that legislative processes are very different from the judicial process, I see both as part of the common enterprise of governing the future wisely. And because of the difficulties inherent in producing a text that controls, over time and in a changing world, the outcome of concrete cases dealing with all aspects of the relation of governments to their constituent parts and of governments to individuals, I see law making as an inevitable and authorized function of adjudication.

So much then for originalism and its authority. The conclusion: not a promising approach to interpreting the Constitution. When we turn to the usefulness of the doctrine in controlling the judiciary—in keeping it in check—we find that originalism is not effective in the way its advocates seem to believe.

It is hardly surprising that most Americans worry some about controlling the judiciary. Start with the proposition that all aspects of government must be checked if tyranny is to be kept at bay, add to this the federal judiciary's immunity from electoral accountability and its power of judicial review, and you would be foolish ever to let down your guard. This will be so even if you recognize that there are substitutes in the judicial process for representation and electoral accountability, that majority rule is one method among many for reaching important political decisions, and that the regulation produced by constitutional adjudication is often far from final.

Today's originalists seem to worry more than most Americans do about government by the judiciary and the need to check the Court. The ideas behind their concern, which require some investigation, present two sets of problems. The first is closely related to what I have been discussing in the examination of authority I have just concluded.

Originalists believe that if judges are not limited to text and the intention of the founders when interpreting the Constitution, they cannot be effectively checked: they will inescapably convert their personal preferences into constitutional law, and they may bring about dramatic social and political change through constitutional interpretation. These two fears are analytically discrete, for judges may let their personal preferences interfere with their interpretation even if they do not prefer social change but rather prefer the status quo.

I shall undertake to demonstrate that originalism does not itself provide the strong protection from judicial reliance on personal preference that its advocates say it does. And I shall show that judicially mandated change of a dramatic sort is consistent with originalism.

With respect both to the influence of personal preference on constitutional interpretation and to the effecting of dramatic social change through originalism, consider Justice Hugo L. Black, a member of the Supreme Court from 1937 to 1971. However one evaluates historically his vast and important contribution to constitutional law, I think all must agree that he gave the Warren court its substantive direction at least as much as anyone else did. Today's originalists seek to overturn much of the work of the Warren court. Yet Justice Black's approach to constitutional interpretation relied heavily on the language of the document and on the intention of its makers.

Justice Black practiced interpretive review before the term was used (or rather misused) by the profession. He was an originalist. And he was one primarily because he had seen the Court strike down New Deal legislation on grounds that he considered rooted only in the personal preferences of the justices. He sought security in text and original intent from the recurrence of this subjectivity— as originalists do today.

Text and intention were central to Justice Black's view of the First Amendment. Text first. He said: "The beginning of the First Amendment is that 'Congress shall make no law.' I understand that it is rather old-fashioned and shows a slight naivete to say that 'no law' means no law. It is one of the most amazing things about the ingeniousness of the times that strong arguments are made, which almost convince me, that it is very foolish of me to think 'no law' means no law. But what it says is 'Congress shall make no law.' "[18] The Justice went on to say, "I believe [the Amendment] means what it says."

Earlier Black had addressed intention: "It is my belief that there are 'absolutes' in our Bill of Rights, and that they were put there on purpose by men who knew what words meant, and meant their prohibitions to be 'absolutes.' "[19] Maybe; but as with most normative positions based on historical claims, the research of others casts doubt on the Justice's view that protection of speech by the Bill of Rights was intended to be absolute.[20] And the absolutists's position is not made out by appealing to the Amendment's language about expression: "Congress shall make no law . . . abridging the freedom of speech." The contemporary originalist Robert H. Bork is clearly correct when he insists that "[a]ny such reading is, of course, impossible." "Is Congress forbidden," he asks, "to prohibit incitement to mutiny aboard a naval vessel engaged in action against an enemy, to prohibit shouted harangues from the visitors' gallery during its own deliberations or to provide any rules for decorum in federal courtrooms?"[21]

In fact, the language of the Amendment does point to a special status for expression. It creates a stronger presumption against regulation than weaker language would. To say "Congress shall make no unreasonable law . . . abridging the freedom of speech" adds an adjective that weakens a liberty. But the language does not tell a court much. It must look elsewhere to determine the strength of the presumption. And Justice Black knew this. Perhaps it explains his position: "I have to be honest about it. I confess not only that I think the Amendment means what it says but also that I may be slightly influenced by the fact that I do not think Congress should make any law with respect to these subjects. That has become a rather bad confession to make in these days, the confession that one is actually for something because he believes in it."[22]

I do not mean to suggest that Justice Black showed himself to be a willful or dishonest judge by admitting to his personal preference; quite the contrary. But I do mean to suggest that the sources of law to which he restricted himself—text informed by original intent—did not, according to Justice Black's own testimony, preclude his personal preference from influencing his understanding of the Constitution. Originalists believe that limiting judges to text and intent will eliminate personal preference from judicial interpretation. Once again they are wrong.

Justice Black's originalism was also clear with respect to the Fourteenth Amendment, one of the great Civil War amendments imposing constitutional constraints on state action in the racial area and in many other areas as well. Justice Black believed that the draftsmen intended to incorporate the first eight amendments to the Constitution into the first section of the Fourteenth. This would apply to the states the federal Bill of Rights—including those provisions dealing with the rights of the criminally accused.[23]

The Warren Court developed the concept of selective incorporation, which is not quite what Black advocated. But the outcome was much as he had urged.[24] It achieved social change on a very grand scale. It established the Supreme Court as the ultimate arbiter of the substantive content of state criminal procedure. It removed power from state courts and state legislatures. It diminished the importance of state constitutions.

If Justice Black is an example of an originalist, as he certainly is, originalism is a doctrine that cannot be counted on to cabin our least dangerous branch.

Even if originalism were a viable interpretive technique (which it is not), it is not authorized by the Constitution, is based on a misunderstanding of the nature of the judicial process, and fails to control the Supreme Court of the United States. It seems fair to conclude that originalism has little if anything to recommend it. But if not originalism, what?

CHAPTER FOUR

Policing Participation and Restricting Intervention

Early in the last chapter I suggested that contemporary anxiety about the sources of law in constitutional adjudication—of which the interest in original intent is a manifestation—could be traced to the decision in *Griswold v. Connecticut* (1965), in which the Supreme Court held that a state statute making it a crime for married couples to use contraceptive devices violated constitutional "notions of privacy surrounding the marriage relationship." As I remarked, the majority opinion went to extraordinary lengths to avoid the due process methodology that characterized *Lochner*. Because the avoidance of this methodology has also influenced the principal approach to judicial review examined in this chapter, it is useful to look a little more closely at *Lochner* itself.

Lochner v. New York (1905) raised the question of the validity, under the Fourteenth Amendment, of a New York statute fixing maximum working hours for bakery employees. The three opinions are crisp by contemporary standards (one for the Court, holding the statute unconstitutional, and two dissents), which makes them neither gain nor lose persuasiveness. Justice Rufus W. Peckham, who served on the Court from 1895 to 1909, wrote for five Justices. He stated, first, that the "general right to make a contract in relation to his business is part of the liberty of the individual protected by the Fourteenth Amendment. . . . Under that provision no state can deprive any person of life, liberty or property without due process of law. The right to purchase or to sell labor is part of the liberty protected by this amendment, unless there are circumstances which exclude the right." Second, he wrote that such circumstances would seem to include valid state legislation—that is, legislation falling within the rubric of police powers. "Those powers, broadly stated . . . relate to the safety, health, morals and general welfare of the public." Third, "[v]iewed in the light of a purely labor law, with no reference whatever to the question of health . . . [the New York] law . . . involves neither the safety, the morals nor the welfare of the public, and . . . the interest of the public is not in the slightest degree affected by such an act." Fourth, while the law may purport to be a health measure, it is not. "We think that there can be no fair doubt that the trade of a baker, in and of itself, is not an unhealthy one to that degree which would authorize the legislature to interfere with the right to labor, and with the right of free contract on the part of the individual, either as employer or employee." Fifth, other arguments concerning health are frivolous. "Statutes of the nature of that under review, limiting the hours in which grown and intelligent men may labor to earn their living, are mere meddlesome interferences with the rights of the individual."[1] Accordingly, the statute was held unconstitutional.

The first Justice John Marshall Harlan, who served from 1877 to 1911, dissented. He reasoned as follows:

> [I]n determining the question of power to interfere with liberty of contract, the court may inquire whether the means devised by the State are germane to an end which may be lawfully accomplished and have a real or substantial relation to the protection of health, as involved in the daily work of the persons, male and female, engaged in bakery and confectionery establishments. But when this inquiry is entered upon I find it impossible, in view of common experience, to say that there is here no real or substantial relation between the means employed by the State and the end sought to be accomplished by its legislation, ... Nor can I say that the statute has no appropriate or direct connection with that protection to health which each State owes to her citizens, . . . or that the regulation pre-

scribed by the State is utterly unreasonable and extravagant or wholly arbitrary. . . . Still less can I say that the statute is, beyond question, a plain, palpable invasion of rights secured by the fundamental law.[2]

Justice Harlan in effect accepted the majority's concern with contractual liberty, but concluded that the state could interfere with that liberty in the situation at hand.

Justice Oliver Wendell Holmes, Jr. (1902–32), dissented in what has become one of his famous opinions. He saw *Lochner* as "decided upon an economic theory which a large part of the country does not entertain." He made it clear that he did not view the judicial function in constitutional adjudication as having to come to terms with the wisdom or folly of an economic theory reflected in a statute duly enacted by a state legislature. On such questions the Court was to defer to the legislature. A constitution, he said, "is not intended to embody a particular economic theory, whether of paternalism and the organic relation of the citizen to the state or of laissez faire. It is made for people of fundamentally differing views, and the accident of our finding certain opinions natural and familiar or novel and even shocking ought not to conclude our judgment upon the question whether statutes embodying them conflict with the Constitution of the United States."[3]

Holmes's characterization of the Court's opinion as resting on laissez faire economics fits a modern view of the issue raised in *Lochner*. Today most of us would see the New York statute as a protective labor law responsive to a legislative loss of confidence in the private contract regime. We would accordingly be apt to see opposition to the statute as reflecting confidence in the private contract and the underlying economic order with which it is associated; opposition by the Court would thus seem to raise laissez faire economics and the private employment contract to the level of a constitutional requirement.

Yet the majority in *Lochner* purported to see the issue as one of personal liberty. This is not necessarily inconsistent with Holmes's characterization of the Court's approach, or indeed with a present-day analysis if one equates laissez faire economics with personal liberty. Many did and some do. But as Holmes said, the economic theory was widely questioned at the time of *Lochner*. Some believed that employees when dealing individually with their employer had no personal liberty, that the employer had complete control over the terms and conditions of employment. Time changed some to many and ultimately led to the repudiation of *Lochner* and its progeny.

Before the repudiation, however, the programs of the New Deal were placed at risk by *Lochner* and other doctrines (the most important was one that sharply limited congressional power under the interstate commerce clause of the Constitution).[4] President Franklin Roosevelt attacked, most notably with his court-packing plan of 1937 (it encouraged judges over seventy years of age to retire by proposing to add a judge if they did not). This plan failed in Congress, but after it was made the Court did begin to sustain economic regulation. And *Lochner* itself was widely seen as an example of how some powerful old men indulged their personal preferences in the teeth of the people's will, a will manifested through the legislature. The holding and the perceived approach were then explicitly repudiated.[5]

The case of *United States v. Carolene Products Co.* (1938) was an unremarkable example of this repudiation.[6] It stands with others of its time in sustaining economic legislation that probably would have been invalidated less than a decade earlier under the due process clause. Speaking for the Court, Justice Stone made it plain that such legislation was to enjoy a powerful presumption of constitutionality. Judicial review was to be anemic: state law would survive challenge if it had a "rational basis."

The Justice then added a remarkable footnote that is probably the best known of the Supreme Court's marginalia. After suggesting that the presumption of constitutionality might have less force where the Constitution is relatively clear, footnote four of *Carolene Products* goes on as follows:

> It is unnecessary to consider now whether legislation which restricts those political processes which can ordinarily be expected to bring about repeal of undesirable legislation, is to be subjected to more exacting judicial scrutiny under the general prohibitions of the Fourteenth Amendment than are most other types of legislation . . .
>
> Nor need we enquire whether similar considerations enter into the review of statutes directed at particular religious . . . or national . . . or racial minorities . . . ; whether prejudice against discrete and insular minorities may be a special condition, which tends seriously to curtail the operation of those political processes ordinarily to be relied upon to protect minorities, and which may call for a correspondingly more searching judicial inquiry.[7]

If the answers to these questions are yes (they have generally been taken to be rhetorical), the footnote can be seen as "a participation-oriented, representation-reinforcing approach to judicial review."[8] Where the political process fails to function properly, judicial review should be robust; otherwise it should be anemic—that is, no more inquiry of the kind pursued in *Lochner* into the substantive values contained in duly enacted legislation. This is wonderfully attractive. It aims our attention at failures of process rather than of substance in the legislative (or executive) branch. And process is a familiar domain of lawyers and judges. As we saw in chapter 2, some process review permits governmental outcomes, provided only that they are accomplished more scrupulously. In this sense, I argued that judicial review may be less final than is often imagined.

But sometimes process review is troublesome. For example, in Justice Stone's footnote the words "undesirable" and "prejudice" may not reveal themselves easily, indeed perhaps not at all, if a judge is barred from inquiring into the substantive values advanced or curtailed by a statute. Moreover, as Professor Bruce Ackerman of

Yale has persuasively argued, "anonymous and diffuse" minorities may be worse off in the legislative process than the "discrete and insular" ones referred to in the footnote.[9]

In his book *Democracy and Distrust* (1980), however, Professor John Hart Ely effectively discusses the footnote in terms of the malfunctioning of the more majoritarian branches: "Malfunction occurs when the *process* is undeserving of trust, when (1) the ins are choking off the channels of political change to ensure that they still stay in and the outs will stay out, or (2) though no one is actually denied a voice or a vote, representatives beholden to an effective majority are systematically disadvantaging some minority out of simple hostility or a prejudiced refusal to recognize commonalities of interest, and thereby denying that minority the protection afforded other groups by a representative system."[10]

While a malfunction in process may be a good reason for the exercise of judicial review (assuming we can get a grip on what a malfunction means), its absence is not necessarily a good reason for denying review. Are there not substantive malfunctions that require serious judicial review? Is it not the case, for example, that there are areas of individual autonomy and privacy where Government should not intrude without sufficient justification, but sometimes does? Is the capacity of the Court not as great here, and its role not as important, as where the perceived malfunction is one of process?

Do not answer yes too quickly. To paraphrase Alexander Bickel, you may find yourself in bed with voluptuaries of economic due process. Recall that it was in the name of liberty that labor legislation was declared unconstitutional in *Lochner*.

Professor Ely knows this, and he has no trouble giving an emphatically negative "answer" to my questions: "Our government cannot fairly be said to be "malfunctioning" simply because it sometimes generates outcomes with which we disagree, however strongly. . . . In a representative democracy value determinations are to be made by our elected representatives, and if in fact most of us disapprove we can vote them out of office."

While few would suggest that all outcomes with which they disagree strongly are malfunctions, I will suggest that some may be. More importantly for now, there are several difficulties with Ely's "answer" to my questions. They are difficulties that undermine the approach taken in *Carolene Products* insofar as its purpose is to keep judges from making value judgments. And in the minds of some students of the Court, especially originalists, making value judgments means "Lochnerizing," or having judges impose their personal preferences. Ely sometimes refers to this judicial activity as "value impositions."

The first problem with Ely's argument is that the judicial diagnosis of a process malfunction may itself entail a value determination. For example, given the method for selecting U. S. senators, it is far from clear to me how a court in many situations can know whether a legislative apportionment is a malapportionment, unless of course it develops a theory of political fairness. I challenge anyone to develop such a theory without making value determinations. The repudiation of one person, one vote in the selection of our one hundred senators reflects a value determination clearly spelled out in the Constitution. The repudiation by the Supreme Court of similar value determinations in state law itself reflects a very different value determination about the meaning of fairness in our political processes. The Court has held that both branches of a bicameral state legislature—its House and its Senate—must be elected in a way that conforms with the principle of one person, one vote.[11] You won't find the source of this value determination—the source of law—in original intent. Needless to say, that does not mean that I think the Court was wrong; but it is to say that the policing of political participation has problems within it identical to those that so upset the originalists.

Second, the judicial cure for a process malfunction may require judges to make value determinations. Take the First Amendment. As Ely tells us, "Courts must police inhibitions on expression and other political activity because we cannot trust elected officials to do so: ins have a way of wanting to make sure the outs stay out."[12] Agreed. If speech reflects the views of an administration, it does not need judicial protection: no one in authority is apt to stop it. However, it may need judicial protection if the speech attacks those in power.

But when we come to apply the First Amendment to defamation, for example, we find that a court must place a value on reputation if it is to fashion a rule protecting unpopular political expression considered defamatory under state law. The famous case of *New York Times v. Sullivan* (1964), which gives First Amendment protection in many situations to untrue and defamatory statements, may be the correct cure for this process malfunction, but in the line of cases applying and qualifying *Sullivan*, speech sometimes yields to reputation.[13] Where this has occurred, the Court has in effect decided that free expression does not have enough weight to overcome a state's determination that an individual's reputation needs legal protection. Such a decision by the Court requires that the justices come to grips with substantive values and reach judgments about them.

————

Ely is hardly unmindful that under his elaboration of *Carolene Products* judges make value determinations. Among other things he has this to say:

Participation itself can obviously be regarded as a value, but that doesn't collapse the two modes of review I am describing into one. As I am using the terms, value imposition refers to the designation of certain goods (rights or whatever) as so important that they must be insulated from whatever inhibition the political process might impose, whereas a participational orientation denotes a form of review that concerns itself with how decisions effecting value choices and distributing the resultant costs and benefits are made . . . I surely don't claim that the words have to be used thus. . . . I claim only that that is how I am using them, and that so used they are not synonyms.

If the objection is not that I have not distinguished two concepts but rather that one might well "value" certain decision procedures for their own sake, of course it is right: one might. And to one who insisted on that terminology, my point would be that the "values" the Court should pursue are "participational values" of the sort I have mentioned, since those are the "values" (1) with which our Constitution has preeminently and most successfully concerned itself, (2) whose "imposition" is not incompatible with, but on the contrary supports, the American system of representative democracy, and (3) that courts set apart from the political process are uniquely situated to "impose."[14]

Perhaps, then, the raison d'être for a "participational orientation" is not so much that it will control the judiciary, but that it is authorized by the Constitution, properly understood. Judges are empowered to impose participational values, and at least for Ely they should impose them with gusto: *Democracy and Distrust* stands as an elegant defense of the transformation by the Warren Court of American constitutional law through the vindication of participational values.

But problems remain. Yes, the text of the Constitution is concerned with participational values, and it can be understood to authorize judges, in a proper case, to enforce such values. As Ely admits, however, the Constitution is also concerned with other kinds of values, the ones that Ely finds unsuitable for judicial enforcement. Yet if we have judicial review, the First Amendment, for example, must be elaborated. And as I have just demonstrated in discussing *New York Times v. Sullivan*, this requires judges to make substantive value judgments.

I suggest that the desire to limit judges to participational values is influenced by a rather idealized conception of nonjudicial decisionmaking. As I argue in chapter 2, the regular and accepted practices of the legislative branches, congressional staff, and the bureaucracy generally lead to a complex structure of government requiring many individuals and organizations to make "substantive" value determinations. More than a few of these individuals and organizations are not elected. They bring to their tasks qualities different from those of nonelected judges. They are constrained in their decisionmaking in ways different from the ones that constrain judges, and the consequences of their decisions differ too. Expectations ought to be realistic. One who worries about judicial power should ask: judicial power compared to what? In answering that question it is well to remember, after reviewing the work of the House of Representatives, that even there it is difficult to make a strong affirmative case for the discipline of electoral accountability. Money counts, incumbents get it, and they are regularly returned to office.[15]

What this suggests is that not only are distinctions between "participational" and "substantive" values themselves a product of value imputation, but that the judicial imputation of either type of value can be seen as compatible with American democracy.

———

In an important sense the judicial review of *Carolene Products* imposes an obligation on the justices of the Supreme Court that is further removed from the normal task of judges than other approaches to constitutional adjudication: *Carolene Products* requires justices to be political philosophers and to work at a very high level of abstraction. To police participation in what Ely calls "the American System of representative democracy," each justice has to understand, develop, invent (what is the right word?) that system and then be prepared to impose it. When a group loses in the political branches and appeals for redress to the judicial, the courts must decide whether the loss is consistent or inconsistent with representative democracy. What is the starting point for decision? Is it some form of liberal theory? Republican theory? Conservative theory? Social choice theory?

For a court, such a question imposes a task that is different in kind from the sort that a case like *Goldman v. Weinberger* entails. *Goldman* deals with a vital but narrow issue: the free exercise of a religious practice in the military. If you were to make the mistake of thinking about the judge's task in terms of personal preferences, you might think of the Court's decision (if you think it wrong) as the rough equivalent of a narrow constitutional amendment. To understand, develop, or invent the American system of representative democracy is the rough equivalent of having an openended constitutional convention.

Well, perhaps this is hyperbolic: when interpreting the free exercise clause of the First Amendment the Court should not be clausebound; it should attend to the place of religious liberty in American society. But the push of Justice Stone's footnote—the condition precedent to applying that form of judicial review—is often toward stratospheric philosophizing, as it is in reapportionment. High irony this, given the ambition of participational theorists to restrict the role of the Court.

Participational theorists seem to share Bickel's belief that "nothing . . . can alter the essential reality that judicial review is a deviant institution in American democracy." Accordingly, such review should be contained, limited, or channeled. This is accomplished, so they believe, by policing participation not substance. Review that fits the criteria set out in 1938 in Justice Stone's footnote should be searching; elsewhere great deference is to be paid by the Court to the work of electorally accountable bodies. Moreover, participational theorists believe that their approach to judicial review is authorized by the text and structure of the Constitution and that it controls judges by preventing them from imposing their personal values on the nation.

Other approaches brought to the practice of constitutional judging are based in the virtues of authority and control (claimed as well by the originalists) and in a belief in the undemocratic nature of judicial review. One approach lacks nuance but from time to time has had powerful political support, and often distinguished academic and judicial support. It is the approach grounded in across-the-board judicial restraint, and I shall talk a little about it at the end of this chapter. Other approaches, based on the same foundational beliefs and concerns, attempt to discriminate among constitutional questions (as the participationalists do). There are many conflicting positions: robust review should be limited to individual rights; it should be limited to separation of powers or to federal-state relations. And there is the first paragraph of Justice Stone's footnote: "There may be narrower scope for operation of the presumption of constitutionality when legislation appears on its face to be within a specific prohibition of the Constitution, such as those of the first ten Amendments, which are deemed equally specific when held to be embraced within the 14th."

In my discussion of Justice Black in chapter 3 I have pointed out the trouble with the first paragraph of the footnote as a source of law: adjudication involving the Bill of Rights is not dramatically different from adjudication involving less textually explicit provisions of the Constitution. Even the First Amendment is open-textured. It requires a great deal of interpretation. If there is to be deference to electorally accountable departments of government through a presumption of constitutionality, why not defer here as well? After all, legislators are under an obligation to work within the Constitution. A text with more words can be seen as giving more information to them as well as to judges. So why not the same presumption? The question is, how powerful should that presumption be?

Felix Frankfurter, who served on the Supreme Court from 1939 to 1962 and was an active adviser to President Franklin Roosevelt while a distinguished professor at Harvard, was a justice who believed that the presumption of constitutionality should be powerful indeed. He was more or less committed to across-the-board judicial restraint. Throughout his career, Frankfurter was influenced (although never inordinately) by the work of James Bradley Thayer of the Harvard Law School. In 1893 Thayer published an article, "The Origin and Scope of the American Doctrine of Constitutional Law," in which he concluded that the Court should declare an act of Congress unconstitutional only "when those who have the right to make laws have not merely made a mistake, but have made a very clear one,—so clear that it is not open to rational question." Thayer went on: "This rule recognizes that, having regard to the great, complex, ever-unfolding exigencies of government, much which will seem unconstitutional to one man, or body of men, may reasonably not seem so to another; that the Constitution often admits of different interpretations; that there is often a range of choice and judgment; that in such cases the constitution does not impose upon the legislature any one specific opinion, but leaves open this range of choice; and that whatever choice is rational is constitutional."[16]

Thayer rested some of his case on the structure of the Constitution. He seemed to see a strong relation between the scope of judicial review and the judicial nature of the power that the Court exercises. Thayer emphasized that this judicial nature meant that the constitutionality of a statute was generally not considered by the Court for some time. Thayer argued that if the scope of review was meant to be broader, if the Court was to do more than correct "very clear" mistakes, earlier intervention would have been provided for in the Constitution—something in the nature of a judicial council of revision to conform legislation with fundamental law.

I confess that I do not understand this argument. It does not seem to me that there is any relation between the time of review and its purportedly limited scope, let alone a necessary relation. Indeed, the argument seems to run the other way: time and a specific case give the Court an opportunity and a perspective different from those of Congress. Strong deference to the interpretation by Congress of the Constitution mitigates this judicial advantage.

On certain premises, however, a good argument can be made for Thayer's conclusion. The premises are that judicial review is a deviant institution, and that there are no sources of law for interpreting the Constitution except the personal values of the interpreters. Since it is my claim in this book that neither premise is correct, I think Thayer himself has made a very clear mistake. Nevertheless, I do want to insist that the views of the legislature may be of weight in constitutional adjudication, for legislators too are duty-bound to respect constitutional limits. I recognize, of course, that the question of a statute's constitutionality may not be closely attended to by the legislature; indeed that sometimes the approach in the law-making body is to leave a hard constitutional question to the judiciary. These are factors to be taken into account by judges in deciding how strong a presumption of constitutionality (if any) should attach to challenged legislation, and there are many others that I shall address in subsequent chapters. This much seems clear: the answer to the question of how to restrict judicial intervention appropriately will not be found in Justice Frankfurter's across-the-board judicial restraint any more than it will be in the approach to policing participation taken in *Carolene Products*.

PART III

The Common-Law Method

CHAPTER FIVE

Sources of Law and the Process of Adjudication

Questions of where, whether, and how strong a presumption of constitutionality should attach to governmental action are related to questions about both the authority of the Supreme Court when it interprets the Constitution and the control of the least dangerous branch. The relations are of the following sort. Start with the proposition that the Constitution does not easily reveal itself. Often it is open-textured and vague: it is a constitution; it is not a tax code. What then are the appropriate sources of law—the appropriate materials—available in the interpretive enterprise?

In the article he wrote in 1893, James Bradley Thayer sharply distinguished that enterprise from what judges normally do, and thereby placed himself in opposition to John Marshall, who had emphasized the similarity between judicial review and other forms of adjudication. Thayer's strong presumption of constitutionality—his "very clear mistake" rule—can find some support in the countermajoritarian nature of the Court (remarked earlier). It also can find support in doubts about the authority of the Court to employ the normal sources of law used by courts in adjudication. Thayer himself deduced this lack of authority from the nature and structure of the Constitution: its nature is political, and its structure brings the Court into the interpretive process only where there is a case or controversy. The Court is not a council of legislative revision. If it were, perhaps it would be permissible for it to employ standard techniques of interpretation that rely on normal sources of law for elaborating a text. But it acts only after Congress has made its policy choices, and given the Constitution's political nature the Court must be extremely deferential to the congressional decision. That is the limit of its authority.

Doubt about the Court's authority to engage in more robust review, moreover, would surely be fed by a belief in the proposition that the standard judicial methods of interpretation invite judges to impose their own values on the nation.

In this portion of the book, I shall maintain that what might be called a common-law method of judicial review best explains American constitutional law, and that while far from perfect it is normatively superior to rival approaches. My plan is first to review briefly the process of adjudication, with special attention to the Supreme Court. This review draws on chapter 1 and can be thought of as an inquiry into the method of generating the materials to be used in interpretation; that is, the sources of law. Second, I shall look at one aspect of the sources of law question from a substantive perspective, as contrasted to a methodological perspective. But even here I shall not be free from methodology. For my attention will in part be directed toward Alexander Bickel's search for the purpose of judicial review; one that is bound up with the process of adjudication, as I think it must be. In *The Least Dangerous Branch* Bickel writes: "The search must be for a function which differs from the legislative and executive functions; which is peculiarly suited to the capabilities of the courts; which will not likely be performed elsewhere if courts do not assume it."[1] Armed with "a function that differs from the legislative and executive functions," I shall be prepared to say something about substance and presumptions of constitutionality in the troublesome area of privacy and abortion.

————————

We begin with John Marshall. In *Marbury v. Madison* he pointed the way. For in holding that the Constitution is law, law to be applied by "the judicial department," Marshall committed the Constitution to a governmental branch that can take the long view because it is removed from electoral politics (this commitment was not necessarily exclusive, but as it turned out it was irrevocable). And he committed the Constitution to the one department of government that many students of law would say finds its authority in the ideal of a rigorous adherence to principle. But what can that mean, given the nature of adjudication?

Principles in law are contextual, they are constructed through the process of adjudication, and they have many sources. While these sources differ in common-law, statutory, and constitutional adjudication, these three types of adjudication have a strong family resemblance. We can learn a great deal about that resemblance by inspecting adjudication and remembering some of its features. Out of many features I shall again call attention to just a few that I discussed in chapter 1. My object is to place substantive interpretation—the derivation and elaboration of principles—in the context of constitutional adjudication. It is a context different indeed from others where interpretation is practiced. Reading poetry, directing a play, understanding and teaching the Bible are examples of interpretive projects that occur in contrasting environments. There are similarities between constitutional interpretation and interpretation as it is practiced elsewhere, but because the legal environment is so different from other environments, the similarities are dominated by the differences.

Recall first that in adjudication various groups interpret the Constitution in accordance with the understanding of their membership. Their lawyers argue to establish and through governmental power to impose on the nation that understanding, the understanding of their clients. Other lawyers, representing other interests, argue for a different interpretation, one shared by their clients. Constitutional principles and legal sanctions emerge from this dynamic, adversarial process; in this methodological sense, the process itself is a source of law.

This process, resulting as it does in the imposition of sanctions, is different from most interpretive processes. Indeed where else does an interpretive process bestow authority on officials to take away property and even life? And this authority, like the prospect of execution, concentrates the mind wonderfully. The participants in appellate adjudication—the lawyers and the judges—are bound to be fully aware of, and influenced by, the consequences of their activity.

Second, recall that in constitutional adjudication the claims the advocates make are about the text of the Constitution and how that text has been and should be interpreted. This entails client-interested explanations of such matters as prior decisional law, historical context, and present circumstances. It entails an appeal to tradition and aspiration—an appeal to values and morality. All these matters are deeply contested, but the contest is itself constrained by the process of adjudication. The players are members of an interpretive community. They remember their professors exhorting them to argue "like a lawyer," and they know that those before whom they contest will listen only to certain types of arguments.[2]

Often the effort of the advocate is to depict these contested matters in the least challenging, most conventional of ways; that is, normal, common, public ways, ways that are consistent with the aspirations, morality, and general understandings of the population. If you were an advocate, wouldn't you want to present your client's claim in a way that was as close as possible to what you took to be the conventional understanding of relevant materials? Even such an understanding must be explained and applied, extended, and perhaps, at least to some extent, transformed. You want your client to win, and it is apt to help if you can depict the client's values as public values or, to put it the other way round, if you can interpret public values so that they encompass the client's claim.

Your adversary will do the same.. Both of you are trying to persuade disinterested—here in the sense of not client-interested—judges who will render a decision disposing of the dispute and write an opinion regulating the future.

Third, at the appellate level a majority decision requires the assent of other judges to the reasoning of its author. Indeed, before an author is selected to write, the members of a court must vote on the case. There are many reasons why voting itself is an important part of the process that may shape the principle on which a decision turns.

Consider the Supreme Court. In the contest for votes, it would appear that in addition to reasoned arguments justices have used personal flattery and emotional appeals, and have even traded votes.

Evidence also suggests that a justice may vote with the majority even while disagreeing with its treatment of the case, and then bargain to influence the Court's opinion. Justices also may threaten to write dissenting or concurring opinions or try to form voting blocks to influence opinions. In cases of extreme importance, justices may assent to the majority opinion to make it unanimous, even if they have some misgivings about it.

Once a vote is taken, the opinion is assigned. If part of the majority, the Chief Justice assigns the opinion; otherwise the assignment is made by the senior Associate Justice who shares the majority view. The ability to assign the opinion is itself a sometimes powerful opportunity to influence the eventual outcome. For example, the opinion may be assigned to a justice who does not hold firm views, but who has a vote that is needed for a majority. The task of writing often persuades an equivocal author, and the draft majority opinion is the starting point for draft dissents and concurrences.

The opinion writing process is a product of conflict and compromise. Majority positions may turn into minority positions and back again. Opinions are written and changed in an attempt to get votes and in response to the views and arguments of other justices. Justices may circulate draft dissenting and concurring opinions for the purpose of shaping the final results. And these tactics do work, at least some of the time.[3]

What all this means is that in the voting and writing processes, negotiation plays a role in formulating constitutional principles. In this methodological sense, then, negotiation too is a source of law.

Fourth, principles once established through this process have a life of their own. For it is emphatically the nature of the judicial process that principles be applied in as disinterested and consistent a fashion as possible. As I observed in chapter 1, both a commitment to the rule of law and broad-based participation in regulating through adjudication require that like cases be treated alike. This process of applying principles in a consistent and disinterested fashion is an interpretive process itself subject to the other features of adjudication—the inescapably political features—that I have just described.

Some students of adjudication find an intolerable tension between advocacy and negotiation on the one hand and the ideal of a consistent, disinterested application of principles on the other. This is particularly true if one imagines the judicial task—and many students seem to—as performed by a lonely scholar in a quiet corner of a library. The reality is otherwise, and the student who neglects context initially is bound to be disappointed by the degree of uncertainty in the law. Too often cynicism results from this disappointment, the realization that one's expectations are unrealistically high because one's conception of the enterprise is wrong.

Of course there is tension. The ideal of a rigorous adherence to principle is contextual. Judges are not scholars, critics, or priests. While it is not quite true that the process makes the product, neither is it false that it does, that constitutional interpretation is the practice of nonpartisan, principled politics.

In practice law changes, after negotiation within a court, because of the judges' skeptical receptivity and reserved openness to the claims of various groups—claims shaped and presented by lawyers using legal arguments and trying to win cases. This is the way all law develops through adjudication, including constitutional law.

———

For all its similarity to other forms of law development, however, the development of constitutional law through adjudication is distinctive. One or more agencies of government have acted, and in acting they have explicitly or implicitly interpreted the Constitution as permitting them to do what they have done. It is the correctness of this interpretation that is being challenged. This is why it is so important to get straight the Court's special function, to locate its interpretive strength. And surely it is now clear why this is so. It is not simply because judicial review is undemocratic. It is because judicial review sometimes is more final, more difficult to change, if change is seen as desirable, and because the process of adjudication is hardly a model of pure reason. Like all governmental processes, it has a political dimension. Unless there is an interpretive strength in the politics of appellate adjudication—a special function—judges ought to be modest and respect the product of other political processes.

The task of locating the Court's special function is not easy, but in chapter 2 we made progress. Let's look again, and again begin with Bickel's reminder "that many actions of government have two aspects: their immediate necessarily intended, practical effects, and their perhaps unintended or unappreciated bearing on values we hold to have more general and permanent interest."[4]

At least in individual rights cases, it is just these values that lawyers invoke in behalf of their clients. In *Goldman v. Weinberger,* for example, the arguments were about the value of religious freedom and its free exercise in the armed forces. The constitutional text to be interpreted or reinterpreted by the Supreme Court was the First Amendment—the Air Force had acted on the basis of a congressional authority that was itself based on implicit or explicit constitutional interpretation. To cite another example, the value of equal protection of the law, textually lodged in the Fourteenth Amendment, was at issue in the gender cases surveyed in chapter 1. In each of those cases other branches of government, either state or federal, had explicitly or implicitly interpreted the Constitution and decided that it was permissible to make distinctions turn on gender.

The "values we hold to have more general and permanent interest," some of which the lawyers representing Goldman said had been improperly disregarded by the air force, and which Weinberger's lawyers said had been properly respected, are the source of legal principles. These values must be weighed by the lawyers and judges who take part in the process of adjudication. Their weight changes from one generation to another as they are used in interpreting constitutional text. They are the values that form a public morality, the ethical principles, the ideals and aspirations that are widely shared by Americans—even as their application is deeply contested.

Of course legislators are often professionally concerned with this public morality. They are concerned with interpreting public values, with shaping and contributing to them. One cannot begin to think about statutes dealing with the death penalty, for example, without coming quickly to such issues. But consider the environment in which legislators function. It is often hard for them to resist pressure from their constituents who react to particular events (a brutal murder, for instance) with a passion that conflicts with their more general, permanent, shared values. While we rarely lynch people today, legislators frequently adopt a "lynching" frame of mind that is deeply at odds with our moral ideals. Nor is it an easy matter for legislators to interpret public values when there are well-organized interest groups insisting on their own self-interested positions.

The clients of lawyers are also self-interested. But the lawyers are arguing to judges who are disinterested—meaning here that they are not electorally accountable, are not paid by clients, and if on the Supreme Court are rarely concerned with professional advancement. And the lawyers are arguing specifically about the effect of governmental action on interests claimed to be constitutionally protected. These interests have a textual basis. The constitutional text has been elaborated through the process of "litigating elucidation." The lawyers' arguments are made in terms of that prior elucidation. The adversarial effort is to distinguish or support, undermine or contract, extend or overrule the prior law by reinterpreting its meaning and basis; that is reinterpreting the language, history, and public values that are the sources of law.

The process of constitutional interpretation in the legislature usually takes a different form. Often it is not at all explicit. But even when constitutional issues are addressed, they are generally one small factor considered along with many others in a larger legislative project directed toward promulgating policies or developing a program to regulate an area of life, at wholesale and prospectively. In the situation that brought about *Goldman v. Weinberger,* for example, one can imagine that Congress empowered the Pentagon to develop rules of dress with at most a passing concern having been expressed by either entity about the free exercise of religion; presumably Congress acted at the behest of the Pentagon after listening to its spokespersons and to no one else. Another example is provided by legislation passed in 1988 aimed at reducing America's drug problem: while noting that drug dealers and users had due process interests, Congress failed to give these interests careful consideration. Due process interests were seen as obstacles to an effective policy that were to be overcome as summarily as possible.

Courts also regulate the future, and the Supreme Court in particular must be more concerned with the regulatory aspects of its work than with the dispute resolution aspects. But it is not formulating a drug policy or producing a dress code on the basis of information that is developed in legislative processes, where the public interest contends with many private interests, and where concern for the individual may receive inadequate attention. The Court has before it a well-defined controversy, one that is rich in the details of the particular and that sharpens the constitutional interests that may have suffered as a result of the formulation or implementation of a legislative program. In giving effect to these interests in their present context through the processes we have examined, the Court must articulate the principles used to elaborate text in the past, principles that often acquired their weight in public morality and that must be reinterpreted in terms of a contemporary understanding of that morality.

What do I mean by principles acquiring their weight in public morality? I can answer this by asking you to consider again the gender discrimination cases discussed in chapter 1. There we saw that the distinctions legislatures have been permitted to make between women and men when enacting regulatory statutes have turned on changing national attitudes about the importance of gender equality. These attitudes reflect widely shared public values. They constitute a public morality.

The constitutional principle requiring that equality be considered by the Court is derived from the text of the equal protection clause, its weight from what I have just described as public morality. This way of viewing the issue is reflected in the case law: because the goal of equality between the sexes has a more prominent place in our current national catalogue of public values than it did in the past—because it weighs more in our public morality—states no longer may justify gender distinctions on grounds of mere rationality, as they did before. "[C]lassifications by gender must serve important governmental objectives and must be substantially related to achievement of those objectives."[5]

The weight of public morality as a source of law, along with other sources of law (language, precedent, structure, and history), is determined by the Court through the process of adjudication. As we have seen, this process results in a unique form of interpretation. But like all interpretation, it is creative. It would be wrong to think of it as the equivalent of digging for gold and finding the ore. Among the participants in adjudication—the lawyers and judges—there must be a constructive reworking of the materials that constitute the sources of law used in elaborating the text. Interpretation is interactive. The participants working with the appropriate materials make law; but they are constrained by the methodological and substantive conventions of adjudication.

When the attention of the legislature has been focused primarily in formulating a program, as was the case when Congress passed the act of 1988 concerning drugs, courts should not assume that the legislature has carefully interpreted the Constitution. It follows that a presumption of constitutionality on the part of the courts would be misplaced. Given the comparative disadvantage of the legislature (through inability or unwillingness) to attend to a program's effect on constitutional interests, judicial review should be robust. Legislative advantage is in the general design of the program and not in its constitutional side effects. Sometimes, however, this distinction between the program and its impact on constitutional interests is elusive. Regulation in the privacy area provides an example.

But we must stop and back up before we can go forward to the privacy area and examine some of the applications and difficulties with the position I am developing about presumptions of constitutionality on the one hand and public values or morality on the other.

First, let me make clear that it is only through example, and in context, that we can get a feel for this concept of public morality that I am inviting you to see as a source of constitutional law, and that some commentators have suggested is nothing more than the value imputation of the constitutional interpreter.[6]

Second, public morality, as I have suggested, is one source of law among many used to interpret the Constitution. Its role has been central, for example, to the jurisprudence of the Supreme Court in the area of capital punishment. It has been a source of law for determining when the death penalty constitutes "cruel and unusual punishment," as these words are used in the Eighth Amendment. Other sources of law in constitutional adjudication used to interpret the text are constitutional structure, history and precedent.

Some believe it makes no sense to think of public morality as a source of law for protecting individuals or groups against the will of the majority as that will is manifested in legislation. For while legislation itself may not always represent the will of a present majority, at other times it does; and while public morality and public values, "values we hold to have more general and permanent interest," are often not the same as the action positions of a present majority, sometimes they are.

Consider as an example the recent Supreme Court decision striking down the conviction of a person who violated state law by burning an American flag as an act of political protest. The Court held by a vote of 5 to 4 that the conviction was an abridgment of speech banned by the First and Fourteenth Amendments.[7]

The decision led to lopsided votes of condemnation in the House and Senate, the passage of a federal statute (itself later held unconstitutional) aimed at protecting the flag, and a quick, unsuccessful call by the President for a constitutional amendment—a call that he subsequently renewed without success.

I think the Court's decision was correct for reasons rooted in the purpose and development of the law of free expression. But because of the powerful symbolic significance of the flag, I would be hard put to defend the Court in terms of public values as such. Indeed, in many areas of constitutional law the role of public values or morality is limited. Structure, history, and precedent serve as presumptive vetoes over legislation aimed at restricting speech, interfering with religion, and distinguishing among people on the basis of their race. But—and it is an important but—public morality may have a role even where other sources of law are central. In the first place, it may assist a court in its interpretive task of determining how to deal with the weight of a presumption of unconstitutionality. An example is provided by the defamation cases (discussed briefly in chapter 4) in which free expression conflicts with the protection of a person's reputation.

In the second place, public morality may have a role after the fact. Constitutional decisions must be politically digestible. If they are not they will not survive, and public morality can influence political digestibility. I address this question in part IV.

But in the area of substantive due process (or, if you prefer, constitutional privacy), public morality is the workhorse of interpretation, and *Griswold v. Connecticut* is the beginning of contemporary law.

Let us hypothesize that in 1960 a state had enacted a statute very different from the one eventually struck down in *Griswold v.*

Connecticut (1965); one that made plain in its preamble that slower population growth was its goal and that adduced reasons relating to the state's environment and economy for such a policy. There would have been little room for the Court to question the validity of the statute's purpose. If, however, the means deployed in the hypothetical statute to achieve its goal had been to make it a crime for married persons to have sexual intercourse "between the tenth and twentieth day after the onset of the female partner's last menstrual period," this would have raised an easy constitutional question, a question of personal liberty under the due process clause. The Court would have had to ask itself whether such a restriction offended public moral standards, and if it did (as it seems to me it clearly would have done), whether constitutional doctrine, interpreted in light of these standards, sustained or invalidated the legislation.

Notice, however, that in implementing its policy the legislature could not possibly have failed to consider the constitutional questions, for it could not possibly have ignored public moral standards (indeed it must have undertaken to have "read" them), to have interpreted public values, to have shaped and contributed to them. But whatever the standard of deference to the legislature ought to be, if there is judicial review this statute is unconstitutional. My claim is that this is an example of a very clear legislative mistake. Indeed, I constructed the hypothetical statute to require invalidation even if judicial review were as anemic as Thayer would have it when the constitutionality of a federal law is before the Court.

Griswold v. Connecticut is more complicated than the hypothetical statute. On the one hand, the purpose of the Connecticut statute was to regulate morals; on the other, the means established to effectuate that purpose were less clearly offensive to public morality. The statute provided that "[a]ny person who uses any drug, medicinal article or instrument for the purpose of preventing conception shall be fined not less than fifty dollars or imprisoned not less than sixty days nor more than one year or be both fined and imprisoned."[8] Here, as with the hypothetical statute, the legislature must have been fully engaged with the moral aspects of the legal issue that eventually came before the Court. Under these circumstances, and having in mind the differences between the legislative and judicial processes, how robust should judicial review be? Here temporal considerations must be addressed.

My claim is that because *Griswold* was decided in 1965 and the challenged statute was enacted in 1879, judicial review should rightly have been robust. The passage of time should have eliminated any deference that the Court might have paid toward the legislature's interpretation of public morality. In other words, the responsibility of the Court in *Griswold* was similar to the one it would have had in a situation where the legislature had been concerned with developing a program and had given only passing attention to the consequences of the program's implementation on the constitutional interests of individuals. I shall try to support this claim as we try to place ourselves in 1965 and work out the appropriate holding for the Court in *Griswold*.

In an earlier chapter I examined the Court's opinion holding the Connecticut statute in *Griswold* unconstitutional. The majority opinion was written by Justice William O. Douglas, who served on the Court from 1939 to 1975. According to the second Justice John Marshall Harlan (1955–71) the Connecticut statute, which he too believed was unconstitutional, embodied a "moral judgment [of the Connecticut legislature in 1879] that all use of contraceptives [including use by married couples] is improper."[9]

In 1965, the year of *Griswold*, the moral judgment contained in the statute would seem on analysis to be inconsistent with prevailing public values. As I have argued, the task of the Court is to make such an analysis and connect it with constitutional doctrine. If we are to have judicial review (and in chapter 2 I attempted to demonstrate that judicial review is constitutionally authorized), so much is required from the Court. The analysis cannot, however, satisfy people who demand mathematical exactness: they are bound to find all law disappointing.

The place to begin analysis is a statement in Justice Harlan's opinion that "the intimacy of husband and wife is necessarily an essential and accepted feature of the institution of marriage, an institution which the State not only must allow, but which always and in every age it has fostered and protected." This intimacy resists standardization through a detailed official code of behavior and only the most general legal controls may be placed on it. Enormous discretion for working out the particulars of the relationship must belong to each couple. The existence of this discretion—of control by husband and wife over their intimate relations—is a central feature of the general arrangement between the couple and the state at the time of marriage. It is an arrangement that creates a complex of moral as well as legal rights and obligations on the part of the couple and the state, rights and obligations intrinsic to the institution of marriage that change as the institution changes, but that have and retain a logical, internal consistency.

The need for private control establishes the area of liberty (or privacy) granted to individuals in marriage. This liberty imposes two types of moral obligations: one between husband and wife, the other between the couple and the state. Interference by the state with this granted liberty can intrude on the marriage relationship in ways that are profoundly at variance with basic aspects of that institution.

Apart from the personal degradation that would be endured if the Connecticut statute were enforced, we might ask whether the statute did not substantially interfere with a major reason for marriage. While procreation may once have been a sufficient explanation for the institution of marriage and the only officially acceptable justification for sexual relations, this was no longer the case in mid-twentieth century America. Then, as today, an increasingly important part of the reason for marriage—for the establishment of a state-protected institution—was the growth and nurturing of love. And the pursuit of sexual gratification is a vital aspect of love, while the fear of unwanted pregnancy materially reduces the prospects of sexual gratification.

I submit that this description of marriage accurately reflects the public attitudes that prevailed in 1965. But the Connecticut statute was enacted in 1879, and the state legislature must have addressed public attitudes that prevailed then, which surely were different from what they were nearly a century later. Procreation rather than intimate sexual relations then was central to the institution of marriage.[10] In eighty-six years attitudes shifted, public values changed, and the additional weight that public morality attached to intimate relations imposed a greater burden on the state to justify its interference with that aspect of constitutional liberty.

My claim about marriage is of course not a claim that childbearing and childrearing do not remain an important part of marriage. It is rather that other values became increasingly important as well. Nor does my claim fail to recognize that love and sexual gratification exist outside marriage and that they can and do fail to exist within marriage. This is not the point. The point is that the state has undertaken to sponsor one institution that by 1965 had the romantic and sexual relationship at its core (along with other values). This relationship demands liberty in the practice of the sexual act.

As Harlan suggests, the Connecticut statute is therefore an arguably unconstitutional condition on the privileges that flow from a state-supported institution. He writes [remember that this was a generation ago]: "It is one thing when the State exerts its power either to forbid extramarital sexuality altogether, or to say who may marry, but it is quite another when, having acknowledged a marriage and the intimacies inherent in it, it undertakes to regulate by means of the criminal law the details of that intimacy."

To determine whether the ban on the use of contraceptives is indeed an unconstitutional condition in the marriage context requires further rumination and reflection in the project of interpreting public morality. Thus far the argument is that the act of marriage entitles the married couple to a large area of liberty in respect of their love life, and that the Connecticut statute restricts that liberty. The claim is not that there are no limits on liberty.

Let me, then, make some assertions that I submit were clear in 1965: the state would be taken to have broken its moral obligation arising from its relationship to marriage were it to ban sexual intercourse between married couples, regulate the frequency of inter-course, or regulate the day or time of day when intercourse was permitted. And while such hypothetical regulations are distinguish-able from a prohibition on the use of contraceptives, the distinction with respect to the second hypothetical regulation is more apparent than real.

A ban on intercourse would be a clear violation of the arrangement between the state and the couple, and for this reason it is difficult to imagine the simultaneous existence of such a ban and marriage in anything resembling its present form. This would not be true of a statute stipulating the occasions on which a couple's sexual ap-petite might be indulged. Yet such a statute would be deeply incon-sistent and in sharp conflict with the entire concept of the marriage relationship. It would recall the fine print in a contract for the sale and purchase of a used car that totally contradicts the general import of the transaction; it would smack of fraud. And so too does the Connecticut statute, given its potential effect on the love life of the married couple: the ban could dramatically diminish pleasure because of the fear of unwanted pregnancy. There can be no ques-tion that this can impose a major strain on the state-protected relationship.

My claims concerning public attitudes toward intimate relations in marriage are supported by data about contraceptive practices in Connecticut circa 1965. Before the Connecticut statute was invali-dated, legal sanctions were not imposed on married couples who used birth control devices; if they had been, the state legislature might well have changed the law. Moreover, some types of contra-ceptives could be purchased at any drugstore in the state, for al-though the statute made it illegal to use contraceptives, it did not make it illegal to sell them. These facts constituted evidence helpful to the Court's task of interpreting public values in the context of the question before it, namely whether the anti-use statute had be-come unconstitutional in 1965. While various inferences may be drawn from the evidence, and while some common behavior is widely regarded as immoral even by those who engage in it, the evidence of public acceptance of contraceptive practices tended to support the Court's decision. It was better evidence than the existence of a statute that had relevance to prevailing moral views in 1879, but carried little weight so many years later.

If I am correct in my interpretation of public morality, the Connecticut statute was properly struck down. For as Justice Byron R. White wrote in his concurring opinion, there is "nothing in this record justifying the sweeping scope of this statute, with its telling effect on the freedom of married persons, and therefore [I] conclude that it deprives such persons of liberty without due process of law."[11]

Those of you who worry about *Lochner* in my analysis of *Griswold* are of course right. Both are substantive due process cases. But let me quiet your fears. First, while the bulk of decisions from the *Lochner* era were concerned with economic legislation, in two cases a searching review of laws restricting personal liberties was also undertaken. These cases have never been overruled and provided some precedential support for *Griswold*.

In *Meyer v. Nebraska* the Court upset a statute drastically restricting the teaching of "any subject to any person in any language other than the English language." A language instructor "taught [German] in school as part of his occupation." The Court said: "His right thus to teach and the right of parents to engage him so to instruct their children, we think, are within the liberty of the [Fourteenth] Amendment."[12]

In *Pierce v. Society of Sisters*, the Court held unconstitutional under the due process clause an Oregon statute requiring that children could attend only public schools. In defending the right of parents to send their children to private schools, the Court said: "The child is not the mere creature of the State; those who nurture him and direct his destiny have the right, coupled with the high duty, to recognize and prepare him for additional obligations."[13]

My second point is that the problem with *Lochner*, and with many other cases from the same period, was not that the freedom of contract was seen as an aspect of constitutionally protected liberty. Given perceptions about the employer's control over working conditions, the problem with *Lochner* was rather that the Court attached more weight to that liberty than it could justify by an appeal to public values. These values in *Lochner*, *Meyer*, *Pierce*, and *Griswold* were a relevant source of law for elaborating constitutional text through the process of adjudication.

CHAPTER SIX

Public Morality

The Tragic Problem of Abortion

Public values are also relevant to the abortion issue. In examining that issue, my plan is initially to put aside questions of judicial deference to the legislature, to assume that the appropriate style of judicial review is robust. Later I shall raise questions concerning the appropriateness of giving very little weight to legislative judgments about a woman's "liberty interest" (to use the descriptive phrase employed by the Chief Justice in his abortion opinion of 1989). We begin not at the beginning but with *Roe v. Wade*,[1] and in particular with the Court's holding. The Texas statute that was declared unconstitutional in *Roe* was of the strict variety: except to save the life of the pregnant woman, it was a crime to "procure an abortion." The Court held that a pregnant woman has a "fundamental" "right of personal privacy," "founded in the Fourteenth Amendment's concept of personal liberty . . . [which is] broad enough to encompass the woman's decision whether or not to terminate her pregnancy." The right "is not unqualified and must be considered against important state interests in regulation." These interests, however, must be "compelling" if they are to serve as the justification for limiting a "fundamental" right.

The state of course has "an important and legitimate interest in preserving and protecting the health of the pregnant woman . . . and . . . it has still another important and legitimate interest in protecting the potentiality of human life. These interests are separate and distinct. Each grows in substantiality as the woman approaches term and, at a point during pregnancy, each becomes 'compelling.' " The interest in the health of the woman increases during pregnancy because later abortions are more difficult to perform safely. This state interest becomes compelling "in the light of present medical knowledge . . . at approximately the end of the first trimester." "With respect to the State's important and legitimate interest in potential life, the 'compelling' point is at viability." A fetus becomes viable when it is "potentially able to live outside the mother's womb, albeit with artificial aid. Viability is usually placed at about seven months (28 weeks) but may occur earlier, even at 24 weeks."

From this it follows that:

(a) For the stage prior to approximately the end of the first trimester, the abortion decision and its effectuation must be left to the medical judgment of the pregnant woman's attending physician.

(b) For the stage subsequent to approximately the end of the first trimester, the State, in promoting its interest in the health of the mother, may, if it chooses, regulate the abortion procedure in ways that are reasonably related to maternal health.

(c) For the stage subsequent to viability, the State, in promoting its interest in the potentiality of human life, may, if it chooses, regulate, and even proscribe, abortion except where it is necessary, in appropriate medical judgment, for the preservation of the life or health of the mother.

This trimester framework seemed to command the support of a majority of the justices until July 6, 1989, when the Court decided *Webster v. Reproductive Health Services* (which I discuss below). According to an opinion in this case by Justice Harry A. Blackmun, which strongly supported the approach he had fashioned in *Roe, Webster* did not make "a single, even incremental, change in the law of abortion." But if we count noses and assume fixed perspectives, *Webster* did indicate that a majority of the Court was no longer committed to the trimester framework. What this will mean about pregnant women's constitutional rights is unclear. Little light was shed on this question in the two abortion cases decided by the

Court in the summer of 1990. Clear enough, however, is the survival and potential enhancement of the state's two regulatory interests.[2]

While the state's interest in the health of the pregnant woman is important and has led to legislation and litigation since *Roe,* this issue need not be given any detailed consideration here. The central, tragic problem in *Roe* is the conflict between the state's interest in the survival of the fetus and a woman's interest in terminating her pregnancy.

It is natural to think of legislation "protecting the potentiality of human life" as addressing a moral issue directly. While important instrumental or policy reasons may be adduced for such legislation—economic growth, for instance—they are plainly secondary. The state of Texas and many other jurisdictions (some shortly before *Roe v. Wade*) had made their moral judgments on fetal life in the same sense that Connecticut in *Griswold* had pronounced its judgment on the morality of contraception.

In the procedural posture of *Roe,* review of the state's judgment on fetal life was mandated by the plaintiff's claim that this judgment had impermissibly abridged her liberty. Putting to one side any question of judicial deference to the legislature, the issue of first importance for the Court was how to weigh her interest in that liberty. This required that an inquiry be made into the nature of the principle the plaintiff was asserting and that attention be paid to the interest the state had protected.

The Court itself approached the case more or less along these lines. It did not, however, get far. Much of Justice Blackmun's opinion is devoted to a history of abortion and is related only remotely to the task at hand. We are told that the constitutional principle asserted by the plaintiff is an aspect of the "right of privacy," "founded in the Fourteenth Amendment's concept of personal liberty and restrictions upon state action." The Court elaborated: "The pregnant woman cannot be isolated in her privacy . . . . The situation therefore is inherently different from marital intimacy, or bedroom possession of obscene material, or marriage, or procreation or education."

The Court also had this to say:

> The detriment that the State would impose upon the pregnant woman by denying this choice altogether [whether or not to terminate her pregnancy] is apparent. Specific and direct harm medically diagnosable even in early pregnancy may be involved. Maternity, or additional offspring, may force upon the woman a distressful life and future. Psychological harm may be imminent. Mental and physical health may be taxed by child care. There is also the distress, for all concerned, associated with the unwanted child, and there is the problem of bringing a child into a family already unable, psychologically and otherwise, to care for it. In other cases, as in this one, the additional difficulties and continuing stigma of unwed motherhood may be involved.

But this and the citation of a number of cases are all the Court had to say on this branch of the case.

The Court did no better when it undertook to examine the argument the state had advanced to justify its statute prohibiting the plaintiff from terminating her pregnancy. First, a fetus is not a person within the Fourteenth Amendment. Second, the Court does not know "when life begins": it does know that "the unborn have never been recognized in the law as persons in the whole sense." And third, "[i]n view of all this, we do not agree that, by adopting one theory of life [namely, that it "begins at conception and is present throughout pregnancy"], Texas may override the rights of the pregnant woman that are at stake."

With the opinion of the Court as background, let's now see if we can articulate the principle implicated in *Roe*, and then ascertain how powerful it is, how much it weighs, when it conflicts with the state's interest in the potential for human life. My object is not to construct a justification for the holding in *Roe* that proceeds on a theory different from what I take to be the Court's. For example, since abortion law is a restriction on the liberty of women, equal protection is a likely candidate for such an alternative theory. But my ambition here is to understand *Roe* in its own terms.

With this in mind, consider a statute making it a crime for any person to remove another person's gall bladder, except to save that person's life. Assume that the express purpose of the statute is to preserve gall bladders, it being determined that these organs can survive only so long as they are housed within a living person's body.

I think this is an "uncommonly silly law" (as Justice Stewart said of the Connecticut contraception statute). I think also that it is unconstitutional, that it deprives people with diseased gall bladders of their liberty without due process of law.

To be sure, it is bizarre for the survival of sick gall bladders to be of concern to a state legislature, or indeed to anyone (except perhaps for some medical scientists). This means that the liberty interest asserted need not weigh very much to be constitutionally vindicated. All that need be demonstrated is that it is a constitutional interest.

You may have to uphold the gall bladder statute if you deny the existence of substantive due process (that is, deny that the subject matter of state legislation can be tested under the due process clause) and if you contend that the words "due process" in the Fourteenth Amendment require only procedural regularity (that is, if you contend that the phrase "substantive due process" is an oxymoron). If this is your position, you will certainly uphold the statute unless you claim that privacy is not a part of substantive due process and that it has independent constitutional status. But even though most justices and many commentators worry about *Lochner*, they also accept the existence of substantive due process, and the continuing validity of the cases discussed at the end of the last chapter and of *Griswold* and its progeny. Accordingly, it seems a truth generally acknowledged that constitutional law recognizes the existence of a "substantive" liberty interest. This means that my silly and irrational gall bladder statute is unconstitutional.

Now contrast gall bladders to fetuses. It is entirely understandable that a state should be concerned with the survival of the unborn. There is nothing whatever irrational about it. This means that the liberty interest of the pregnant woman who wants an abortion must have sufficient weight—and, as I shall claim, weight in public morality—to overcome a state's rational, if unwise, abortion law.

But before I get to weight, I wish to examine more closely the claim of the person with the diseased gall bladder; the claim is that the statute infringes on the person's liberty. What is the nature of this liberty interest, this principle that is being asserted, and how does it relate to the principle that might support a constitutional right to an abortion?

The person claims the right to be rid of an organ that has caused acute pain and may do so again, and claims further that to be deprived of this right imposes a regimen that is highly uncongenial, and that the mental strain of a potential rupture is psychologically unsettling. The principle to which this claim is being related is one that is commonly recognized, namely that every person has a right (qualified by context) to decide what happens to his or her body.

The point to notice about this principle (and it is of course a principle that can be asserted by a woman claiming a right to an abortion) is that it has nothing to do with the destruction of the diseased gall bladder once it has been removed from the body. In the case of abortion, the principle has nothing to do with the death of a fetus once it has been removed from the womb.

Professor Judith Jarvis Thomson of the Massachusetts Institute of Technology discerned the distinction between the death of the fetus and the right to an abortion before the decision in *Roe v. Wade:*

> [W]hile I am arguing for the permissibility of abortion in some cases, I am not arguing for the right to secure the death of the unborn child. It is easy to confuse these two things in

that up to a certain point in the life of the fetus it is not able
to survive outside the mother's body; hence removing it from
her body guarantees its death. But they are importantly different. . . . A woman may be utterly devastated by the
thought of a child, a bit of herself, put out for adoption and
never seen or heard of again. She may therefore want not
merely that the child be detached from her, but more, that it
die. Some opponents of abortion are inclined to regard this
as beneath contempt—thereby showing insensitivity to what
is surely a powerful source of despair. All the same, I agree
that the desire for the child's death is not one which anybody
may gratify, should it turn out to be possible to detach the
child alive.[3]

It should be observed moreover that since the principle we are
considering does not support an independent claim to "secure the
death of the unborn child," there is considerable logic in the decision
by the Court in *Roe* to fix on the onset of viability as the point at
which substantial state regulation is permissible. At that point, and
quite apart from how one counts fetal life, the woman may still
plausibly claim that she wants the fetus removed. She has no claim,
however, to a procedure that entails the destruction of the fetus if
there is a procedure available that does not destroy it. At a minimum, therefore, the state must be able to insist on the use of such
a procedure.

Society's clear interest in the well-being of a fetus that can live
apart from its mother, however, suggests that the state can do more.
Roe undertakes to prescribe what more the state can do in the "stage
subsequent to viability." It tells us that in most cases the well-being
of a viable fetus outweighs the woman's right to decide what happens
in or to her body. I shall return shortly to the significance of viability
in the context of *Webster* and Justice Sandra Day O'Connor's earlier
assault on the trimester framework of *Roe*.

Our task is now to determine whether *Roe* is right about the
weight it assigned to the principle or liberty interest of the mother,

for we have determined that if it is sufficiently weighty it could support a woman's constitutional claim to an abortion.

_____

Assume for a short time the validity of the position taken by Texas in *Roe*, namely that "life begins at conception and is present throughout pregnancy." Does the acceptance of this assumption (or its rhetorically more provocative version that the "fetus [embryo, fertilized ovum] is a person from the moment of conception") necessarily conclude the abortion issue? This is the question to which Professor Thomson attends in her short and splendid article from which I have just quoted. She has a good deal to say, all of it is interesting, and some of it is important to a proper understanding of *Roe*.

Given this assumption about fetal life (which Thomson makes for the purpose of the argument even though she does not believe it), Thomson wisely declines to defend an unqualified right to abortion. Her argument, nevertheless, is heroic: some abortions, she says, are justified by resort to the principle that "the mother has a right to decide what shall happen in and to her body." Her major forensic tool is a vivid analogy:

[L]et me ask you to imagine this. You wake up in the morning and find yourself back to back in bed with an unconscious violinist. A famous unconscious violinist. He has been found to have a fatal kidney ailment, and the Society of Music Lovers has canvassed all the available medical records and found that you alone have the right blood type to help. They have therefore kidnapped you, and last night the violinist's circulatory system was plugged into yours, so that your kidneys can be used to extract poisons from his blood as well as your own. The director of the hospital now tells you, "Look, we're sorry the Society of Music Lovers did this to you—we would never have permitted it if we had known. But still, they did it, and the violinist now is plugged into you. To unplug you would be to kill him.

But never mind, it's only for nine months. By then he will have recovered from his ailment, and can safely be unplugged from you." Is it morally incumbent on you to accede to this situation? No doubt it would be very nice of you if you did, a great kindness. But do you have to accede to it?

Thomson's question is meant to be answered no, and it seems to me that no is the only answer that can be defended by an appeal to our attitudes and practices. Nor do I see how her example can be distinguished from abortion where pregnancy results from rape.

Even if one does not grant this much (and I am sure there are those who will not), some features of Thomson's position are worth noticing. First, the example of the violinist would be very different if you had to be hooked up to his circulatory system for nine minutes rather than nine months. The principle, that one is entitled to decide what happens in and to one's body, must not only be accommodated to other principles but must be flexible enough to tolerate relatively minor violations even for relatively minor reasons. Time is important and so is the nature of the violation. A compulsory vaccination is different on both counts from a compulsory pregnancy.[4]

Second, if you agreed to be hooked up to the violinist's circulatory system, your moral position would of course be dramatically changed. This may seem to diminish the claim to abortion of a woman who becomes pregnant after having consented to inter-course. But her situation is different. While observable differences do not mean that she should prevail if the fetus is assumed to be indistinguishable in any relevant way from the violinist, they do suggest—to the extent it is possible to relax the assumption equating fetal life to the life of a person such as the violinist—that consent counts for less than might have been thought.

The woman may have taken all the precautions she could. Con-traception is not foolproof, and the principle of "assumption of risk" can be pushed too hard. Sexual intercourse is not voluntary in the same way that going to a baseball game or agreeing to be plugged into another person's circulatory system is voluntary. It makes sense to speak of voluntariness in contrast to rape, but confusion on this issue should be carefully avoided. To say that Betty goes to the opera voluntarily, Betty voluntarily has sexual intercourse, and Betty voluntarily eats food is not to say that in each case Betty has exercised the same degree of volition.

On the other hand, even if sexual intercourse were a matter of life and death, as eating is, the woman who became pregnant (but was not raped) is not in the position of the person who has been kidnaped in Thomson's example, for this person probably received no benefit from having been hooked up to the violinist's circulatory system.

I think not only that it is possible to relax the assumption that a fetus is like the violinist, but that the assumption is impossible to maintain. Let me call attention to an attitudinal difference that I believe is quite generally held. To save the life of the mother, we are prepared to accept the death of the fetus. Even Texas provided for this. However, suppose that the fetus is removed and placed in an incubator because it appears that it can live. Two days later it is determined that the mother will die if she does not receive a small blood transfusion. The only blood available that matches hers is that of the infant in the incubator. The infant will survive if it keeps its blood but will die if it gives its blood to its mother, who will then survive. I do not think we are now prepared to kill the infant to save the mother.

Part of the reason may be related to the fact that the principle supporting some abortions does not give the "right to secure the death of [even] the unborn child." We are prepared to accept the death of the unborn child to save the mother, but we are not prepared to accept the death of the infant in the incubator because most of us perceive that the fetus has less of a right to life than the infant does. The infant has as much of a right to life as anyone; indeed, it would not matter if its mother were the President of the United States.

To take another example, we are not apt to be surprised or to think it madness if a person favors the abortion of a badly deformed fetus and at the same time opposes infanticide. This again may be related to the limiting factor in the principle that supports abortion, but it also reflects a difference in attitude toward fetal and infant life. Surely we would be bewildered by a person who favored infanticide and opposed abortion.

The example of the deformed fetus purports to show that its survival counts less than the survival of a deformed infant. It does not purport to say anything about the morality of aborting such a fetus, a question to which I now turn. The claim I wish to make is that if one agrees with the main features of the argument thus far, common sense requires that abortion be permitted here.

Consider the following story: Mary and Jane are identical twins. Mary is married in the summer and goes to Europe on her honeymoon. She becomes pregnant and finds it difficult to sleep. She goes to a physician and is given thalidomide, which helps a great deal. Shortly after, evidence is published of the effects of thalidomide on the development of fetuses.

During the summer when Mary is on her honeymoon in Europe, Jane is at work in New York. While walking alone one afternoon she is assaulted and raped. A month later she discovers that she too is pregnant. The sisters seek moral counsel together.

We can explain to Jane that she would be a very nice person if she carried the fetus to term, but that it is morally permissible for her to have an abortion, even if the fetus is considered "a person from the moment of conception."

Having told this to Jane, what shall we say to Mary? I do not think we can now tell her that it is impermissible for her to have an abortion and at the same time persuade ourselves that we are being fair to her. Nor do I think we have to. We can say to Mary (1) that we do commonly draw an important moral distinction between fetal life and other kinds of human life, (2) that this distinction does not mean that fetal life may be disregarded, but that it does enable us to make other distinctions that in its absence would be morally impermissible, (3) that one such distinction, which has considerable intuitive appeal, counts the survival of a fetus that "would be born with grave physical or mental defect" less than the survival of a normal fetus, and (4) that while the chief appeal of this last distinction rests in a widely held preference for the birth of a healthy child, it also gives weight to the principle that a woman "has a right to decide what shall happen in and to her body." Support for the final point may be found in two observations. First, as a rule it is emotionally more painful for a woman knowingly to carry an unwanted defective fetus than it is for her to carry an unwanted healthy fetus. Second, when she engaged in intercourse, the risk that she would have to carry a gravely defective fetus was knowable, but (if we can argue from a conclusion) it was a risk she did not assume. For in assessing the degree of risk assumed, it is permissible to take into account the degree of volition involved in the act creating the risk in the first place. In this respect, Mary is not Jane; but neither is engaging in sexual intercourse the same as going to an opera.

I have been making arguments by taking note of commonly held attitudes and reasoning from them. This is a way of constructing public morality. It should help judges in their task of deciding how much weight to assign to a pregnant woman's liberty interest in an abortion, the weight, in the abortion context, of the principle that she has a right to decide what happens in or to her body. Put another way, for the Court and the lawyers who argue before it, reasoning from these commonly held attitudes should be an important method for interpreting the values—the public morality—that are a source of law in elaborating the term "liberty" in the Fourteenth Amendment of the Constitution.

Now, observe first that while this approach is concerned with the weight of the principle that supports a woman's claim to an abortion, it is also related to the state's interest in the potential for life. Indeed it is difficult to think about one apart from the other; there is bound to be a tragic conflict between them. The person who wants a diseased gall bladder removed runs into no such tragic conflict, for the state has no interest in the survival of the gall bladder. The nature of the conflict will shortly become clearer, when we investigate such terms as "compelling state interest" and the relation of the word "compelling" to the nature and weight of the principle that supports the abortion claim and other claims that might be based on the same principle.

Second, my arguments do not justify the sweep of *Roe v. Wade*. Nor am I able to do so, although someone following the approach I have used may be able to make more progress. I would be pleased to see that done, for as a legislator I would certainly support the outcome of *Roe*.

———

In my discussion of abortion so far, I have assumed that the Court was not to defer at all to the legislature's decision to limit a woman's right to an abortion. I now want to ask whether this is appropriate. My argument has been that deference is inappropriate in situations where the legislature is concerned with enacting a program of some sort (for example, a war on drugs or a dress code for the armed forces) and is for whatever reason inattentive to the effect the program will have on the constitutional interests of individuals— inattentive, that is, to those values that must always have their weights reassessed, and that "we hold to have more general and permanent interest." The Connecticut statute in *Griswold* was not the work of an inattentive legislature; but it was passed in 1879 and was too old to be considered a reflection of public morality in 1965 on the question of contraception. While the statute could have been repealed, that it had not been did not relieve the Court of its responsibilities. Nor is legislative inaction much of a guide to anything. Inaction can be attributed to innumerable causes; in Connecticut it seems most likely that the statute was not repealed because it was not generally enforced.

Roe does not fit well either. As I have been maintaining, the protection of fetal life is connected too closely with the woman's rights over her body for distinctions to be drawn as easily as they are where the legislative program is a dress code or a war on drugs. With respect to the statute under review in *Roe* we must assume that attention was paid to public morality by the legislative branch, and that its view of that morality was entitled to some respect by the Court. There is certainly room for disagreement as to how much. Many factors must be attended to: one is the question of when the legislation was passed (as in *Griswold*). The Texas statute was old— its language can be traced to 1857—but at the time of *Roe* other states had recently enacted abortion legislation, some quite restrictive, others pro-choice. A companion case to *Roe* involved a contemporary Georgia statute that was less strict than that of Texas but more restrictive than the Court's decision in *Roe.*[5] *Roe* was a decision for the nation, and to the extent that public morality can be teased out of state legislation, the legislation of all states counts. This is some evidence that in 1973 public values were more supportive of abortion than the Texas statute was.

In thinking about public morality and legislation, the history of a statute's enactment can also be important. It may show, for example, that a narrow, well-organized interest group was able to an unusual extent to work its will on legislators concerned primarily with reelection. Legislative history is often not readily accessible to a court. One way of reconstructing it, however, is to do what I have done earlier in this chapter: to take note of commonly held attitudes and reason from them. If abortion legislation departs markedly from the insights provided by this judicial analysis, the Court should discount legislative interpretation of public morality. This means that statutes like that of Texas are much too restrictive; it also means that *Roe v. Wade*, when decided in 1973, went too far.

But if one says this, isn't one failing to give weight to the legislative judgment? Doesn't the Court come out the same way it would if the legislative contribution to public morality were ignored? Perhaps, but this is a matter of degree. The Court should defer when it is in doubt, not when it has confidence in its conclusions. Such confidence suggests legislative failure, and legislatures do fail.

But isn't this the process review criticized in chapter 3? Yes and no. What I criticized in chapter 3 was the limitation of judicial review to considerations of process values. I also expressed concern about a court's ability to know what constituted a process failure without attending to substantive values. These problems are not present as such in *Roe v. Wade.*

———

If one thinks that on balance *Roe* was wrong when it was decided for having gone too far, this does not mean that the decision should be overruled. The Supreme Court's decision is not neutral with regard to the issues of public morality that I have addressed, and later abortion decisions have not been either. The Court has moved massively into a debate, and the terms of the debate are now different from what they were. I shall look some at this debate in the following section and in more detail later.

This much, however, should be said now. The doctrine of adhering to precedent, called stare decisis, is grounded in the principle of treating like cases alike and in important considerations of policy. Stability, in its many different aspects, is often especially important: individuals and institutions use prior decisional law in their efforts to organize the future. And the courts themselves build in related areas on their prior holdings. Thus even when an earlier decision is seen as a mistake, policies may dictate sticking to precedent.

In constitutional adjudication, where nonjudicial change can sometimes be difficult, stare decisis has less of a grip than it does where statutory interpretation or the common law is involved. Nevertheless, prior constitutional decisions are a major source of law.

Assuming that *Roe v. Wade* went too far when it was decided, the justification for modifying little or none of it is complex. The decision in *Webster* in 1989 did weaken the precedential value of *Roe*, but the future of *Roe* remains unclear, and we can expect the Court to be struggling with that future for many years, even as it has in the recent past. I shall try to explain in the next part of this book that the struggle relates to the political digestibility of *Roe*. At this point, however, I want to advance what I take to be a very strong reason why the Court should not depart very much further from *Roe* than it already has.

Before *Roe* the states were free to regulate abortion. There was considerable diversity: state law ranged from the strict Texas statute at issue in *Roe* to strongly pro-choice legislation in New York.[6] Our federal system permits great diversity. Often diversity is good, but sometimes too much of it is very bad, and the abortion area is an example. Before *Roe v. Wade*, a rich woman from Texas could get a legal abortion in New York, but a poor woman from Texas could not afford legality, and illegality too often led to tragedy.

As an original proposition, this consequence of the diversity of federalism is difficult to use as a ground for the decision in *Roe v. Wade*. In many areas of life wealth makes a huge difference, but legislation generally does not have to be especially sensitive to this difference. There are some specific exceptions. For example, an indigent defendant in a criminal case has the right to have a written transcript of the trial available on appeal. This right, which reflects the special concern of the Court with criminal procedure, rests on equal protection: the indigent defendant has the right to a transcript because the wealthy defendant can pay for one.[7] But wealth is not a so-called suspect classification under the equal protection clause of the Fourteenth Amendment; and since it is not, the Constitution offers little protection to the poor.[8]

If *Roe v. Wade* were to be totally discarded, the constitutionally unbounded regulation of abortion would be returned to the states. It is difficult to predict the consequences of such an event: *Webster* galvanized the pro-choice forces, which in turn fomented chaos among pro-life politicians before stiffening the resolve of some of them. But it does seem likely that substantial legal diversity would result if *Roe* were overturned. Indeed, by March 1990 the territory of Guam and the legislature of Idaho had passed extremely restrictive abortion statutes. (The Idaho statute, however, was vetoed by the governor and did not become law. And the Louisiana legislature followed suit that summer.)

If diversity of state abortion laws were constitutionally permitted, it would have a disproportionate adverse impact on poor women, and this alone supports stare decisis. The doctrine of stare decisis rests heavily on policy considerations, on the consequences of departing from precedent and establishing a new regime. Those consequentialist concerns may not have much affirmative force in the fashioning of new rules where previously the Constitution was not thought to apply, but along with the principle of deciding like cases alike, these concerns are the foundation on which stare decisis rests.

Consider this from a related but slightly different perspective. Ideally an institution engaged in regulating—in ordering the future wisely—should look at all the consequences of its actions. When the Court regulates through judicial review it sometimes cannot do this, because it lacks the authority to test legislative action by certain criteria. But when it is examining its own precedents, there is no such lack. Indeed, stare decisis places the Court under an obligation to act as wisely as possible, to consider all the consequences of overruling its own interpretation of the Constitution. This requires that judicial attention be paid to the disproportionate impact that overturning *Roe* would have in some of the nation's fifty states and its several territories on poor women—namely, the probable increase in deaths caused by back-alley abortions.

———

Since 1973 the Supreme Court has had many occasions to pass on the constitutionality of legislation aimed at regulating abortion. Until *Webster* in 1989 the Court had been protective of a woman's right of choice, apart from the question of public financing (funds may be provided for delivering babies but withheld for terminating pregnancies).[9] I think it is fair to say that *Webster* extended the ability of states to withhold public financing, by sustaining a Missouri law that prohibited public employees from assisting in an abortion and public facilities from being used for an abortion, except where necessary to save the life of a pregnant woman.

After *Roe* and before *Webster*, the Court had generally invalidated regulations purportedly justified by concern for the woman's health or her need to know about abortion procedures and fetal development, as well as regulations requiring the consent of the woman's male partner.[10] *Webster* did not change this. But when one considers together the plurality opinion in *Webster* written by Chief Justice Rehnquist and joined by Justices Byron White and Anthony M. Kennedy, the opinion by Justice Antonin Scalia calling for the flat overruling of *Roe*, and opinions in earlier cases written by Justice O'Connor, it becomes clear that abortion law is unstable.[11] After 1973 state regulation of abortion had to be consistent with the trimester framework established by *Roe*. One way or another Justices Rehnquist, White, Kennedy, Scalia, and O'Connor have rejected that framework. And without it, precedents are at risk.

The risk is especially great if the state's interest in potential human life is considered "compelling" throughout pregnancy. For this is another way of saying that the woman's right is less of a shield against restrictive state regulation than the Court in *Roe* said it was. Recall that in *Roe* the Court held that this state interest became compelling at viability.

The plurality opinion in *Webster*, while specifically rejecting the trimester framework of *Roe*, did not specifically describe the quality of the State's interest. It specifically omitted a statement that the interest in potential human life is compelling throughout pregnancy. But this is probably because the opinion called the woman's right simply a "liberty interest" and declined to describe it as "fundamental." "Fundamental" is the word used by the Court in *Roe*. By definition, a fundamental right has weight; to overcome it, it would seem that a state must show that its interest in regulation is very substantial indeed. It is not clear in the abortion context what a state must show to overcome a woman's "liberty interest." But it is clear that that interest has greater weight in public morality today than it did before *Roe v. Wade*, and that at least part of the reason for this is the *Roe* decision itself.

At any rate, *Webster* itself was no great surprise. First of all, numerous efforts have been made to overturn *Roe* on the nonjudicial front. These have ranged from the proposing of constitutional amendments to the bombing of abortion clinics. The political process has been actively engaged. In part IV, I shall explore this engagement and its relation to the development of constitutional law. If one puts to one side the flag-burning issue, which is special in that it is isolated and contained, it seems fair to say that in the latter half of the twentieth century only the school desegregation case *Brown v. Board of Education*[12] has had larger public repercussions than *Roe.* Perhaps the school prayer decisions come closest to it in their impact.[13]

In the second place, since 1973 the justices on the Court who accounted for the majority in *Roe* have diminished in number, and two of those who dissented—White and Rehnquist—have remained. Accordingly, well before *Webster* the decision's future was in considerable doubt. The Solicitor General, the chief government advocate before the Court, asked for the reversal of *Roe,* and its framework was sharply questioned by Justice O'Connor, who was not a member of the Court in 1973. She wrote a separate, and carefully restricted, opinion in *Webster* because she thought the Missouri statute was constitutional under *Roe* and the abortion funding cases. Here, from a dissenting opinion, is some of what she said earlier about *Roe* and the state's interest in the survival of the fetus:

> In *Roe,* the Court held that although the State had an important and legitimate interest in protecting potential life, that interest could not become compelling until the point at which the fetus was viable. The difficulty with this analysis is clear: *potential* life is no less potential in the first weeks of pregnancy than it is at viability or afterwards. At any stage in pregnancy there is the *potential* for human life. Although the Court refused to "resolve the difficult question of when life begins," . . . the Court chose the point of viability—when the fetus is *capable* of life independent of its mother—to permit the complete proscription of abortion. The choice of viability as the point at which the state interest in *potential* life becomes compelling is no less arbitrary than choosing any point before viability or

any point afterward. Accordingly, I believe that the State's interest in protecting potential human life exists throughout the pregnancy.[14]

Justice O'Connor's last sentence may be correct, but it does not mean that the Court was wrong in *Roe* when it held that the beginning of viability is the point at which the state's interest becomes compelling. First, do we not generally feel sorrier when a woman miscarries late in her pregnancy than we do when she miscarries early on? And does not the woman feel a greater loss? While both of these feelings are complex—they have to do with the burden of pregnancy and the shattered expectation of birth—one element is the increasing value that we attach to the life of the organism in the womb between conception and delivery. I say "we." I know that some of us do not have feelings related to time: eight minutes or eight months is the same. But few if any public values are held by everyone, and the distinction I am urging does seem widely shared. That we use different terms to describe the organism in the womb— zygote, embryo, fetus—tells us something about time and the value we place on the organism's survival. This relation between time and value probably will deepen when American women are able to obtain and use RU-486 (the French abortion pill that induces a miscarriage early in a pregnancy). Public practices tend to support public values and vice versa.

This suggests that because we are concerned with public values, it is reasonable to see a connection between the duration of a pregnancy and the degree of the state's interest in preserving the life of the organism in the womb. It does not in itself suggest that the moment when the fetus becomes viable is the salient point at which the state should constitutionally be allowed to prohibit abortion. But there is a second reason for thinking that in *Roe* the Court was correct in assigning the importance it did to viability.

The principle that supports a woman's right to an abortion must itself influence judgment about what constitutes a sufficient state interest to defeat the woman's right. Put more generally, the concept of a compelling state interest is related to the nature of the right it trumps. Justice O'Connor, however, seems to think otherwise. It would appear that she sees the state interest and the woman's right as discrete. This might be analytically clean, but it is substantively wrong.

If the woman's right to an abortion included the right to demand the death of the fetus, viability would be irrelevant. It would, as Justice O'Connor insists, be a totally arbitrary point within the nine months of a pregnancy. But the woman has no such right: the death of a fetus from abortion is a consequence of the woman's having exercised a right based on and coextensive with the principle that she may decide what happens in or to her body. Thus, while it is not inescapably true that the state should be prevented from regulating before viability, it is inescapably true that viability is relevant in considering the extent of state power over the abortion decision.

————

The relation of viability to a woman's right to an abortion was not substantially clarified in either the Chief Justice's or Justice O'Connor's opinion in *Webster*. Missouri imposes certain testing requirements before an abortion may be performed past the twentieth week of pregnancy. The object of the tests is to determine whether a fetus is viable. Viability is rarely possible before twenty-four weeks, but it is possible to misjudge the length of a pregnancy's term by four weeks. Justice O'Connor thought that this provision and the other provisions of the Missouri statute properly before the Court were consistent with *Roe*. This meant that the state's interest in potential life was, under *Roe*, "compelling" at the time that viability testing was required.

The Chief Justice agreed, but thought that the testing requirements were inconsistent with some of the language used by the Court to strike down state abortion laws enacted after *Roe*. This led him to reject the trimester framework. But he said little about the nature of the state's interest in potential life before viability. He did say, "[W]e do not see why the State's interest in protecting potential human life should come into existence only at the point of viability [*Roe* did not say it did], and there should therefore be a rigid line allowing state regulation after viability but prohibiting it before viability." He also said that the "Missouri testing requirement . . . is reasonably designed to ensure that abortions are not performed where the fetus is viable—an end which all concede is legitimate— and that is sufficient to sustain its constitutionality." The Chief Justice also cited Justices White and O'Connor, both of whom had said in dissenting opinions in earlier cases that the state has a compelling interest in protecting potential human life throughout pregnancy.[15]

How can a pregnant woman have any right to an abortion if the state has a compelling interest in protecting the fetus throughout pregnancy? Well, perhaps the woman's right is greater. Justice O'Connor, who continues to describe that right as "fundamental," said this: "[J]udicial scrutiny of state regulation of abortion should be limited to whether the state law bears a rational relationship to legitimate purposes such as advance of these compelling interests [health and potential life], with heightened scrutiny [that is, more than a rational or reasonable relationship between regulatory ends and means] reserved for instances in which the State has imposed an 'undue burden' on the abortion decision. . . . An undue burden will generally be found 'in situations involving absolute obstacles or severe limitations on the abortion decision,' not whether a State regulation 'may inhibit abortions to some degree.' And if a state law does interfere with the abortion decision to an extent that is unduly burdensome . . . the possibility remains that the statute will withstand the stricter scrutiny."[16]

Should Justice O'Connor's approach become law and pro-choice political efforts in the states fail to maintain or produce liberal abortion statutes, we can look forward to years of "litigating elucidation." But given the principle that supports a woman's right to an abortion, can it be that the viability of the fetus is unrelated to what constitutes an "undue burden" on the abortion decision? The first quotation that we read from a dissent by O'Connor suggests that that was the Justice's position, and if that is so it was wrong. But perhaps subsequent exposure to the abortion issue through the process of constitutional litigation has changed her mind.

Justice White dissented in *Roe v. Wade.* In 1986 he wrote a major dissent in a case invalidating a Pennsylvania law purporting to regulate abortion within the guidelines established by *Roe.* This was the first case in which the Court had been asked to reconsider *Roe* by the Solicitor General.[17]

One provision of the Pennsylvania law that was struck down "was designed to ensure that a woman's choice of an abortion is fully informed . . . ." In the course of disagreeing with the majority, Justice White quoted with approval the decision by a court of appeals to the effect that the "root premise is the concept, fundamental in American jurisprudence, that '[e]very human being of adult years and sound mind has a right to determine what shall be done with his own body.'" This is of course one way to articulate the principle vindicated by *Roe.* Yet in another portion of his dissent Justice White stated: "The governmental interest at issue is in protecting those who will be citizens if their lives are not ended in the womb. The substantiality of this interest is in no way dependent on the probability that the fetus may be capable of surviving outside the womb at any given point in its development, as the possibility of fetal survival is contingent on the state of medical practice and technology, factors that are in essence morally and constitutionally irrelevant."

Justice White is wrong about medical practice and technology. Viability before twenty-three or twenty-four weeks does not seem to be in the medical or technological cards.[18] He also seems, along with Justice O'Connor, to have forgotten the nature of the principle at stake in *Roe v. Wade* and the way in which the principle and the state interest in potential human life are bound together.

This forgetfulness—if that is what it was—was not especially important in the Pennsylvania abortion case. But Justice White clearly was forgetful, either for the first time or again, in the case of *Bowers v. Hardwick*,[19] in which he wrote for the Court. The case involved the constitutionality of Georgia's sodomy statute (Bowers was the state's attorney general); the Court held for the state by a vote of five to four.

The Georgia statute made sodomy a criminal offense, punishable by imprisonment of one to twenty years. And it defined the crime: "A person commits . . . sodomy when he performs or submits to any sexual act involving the sex organs of one person and the mouth or anus of another." To paraphrase and quote the Court, Hardwick was charged with violating this statute by committing sodomy in the bedroom of his home with another adult male. After the state decided not to prosecute, Hardwick brought a suit in federal court challenging the constitutionality of the Georgia statute. "He asserted that he was a practicing homosexual" and that the statute "placed him in imminent danger of arrest."

Over a sharp objection by the dissenting justices, the Court purported to limit the issue before it: "The only claim properly before the Court . . . is Hardwick's challenge to the Georgia statute as applied to consensual homosexual sodomy. . . . We express no opinion on the constitutionality of the Georgia statute as applied to other acts of sodomy."

I shall address the procedural aspects of this case shortly. It is clear, and should be remarked now, that the issue before the Court would have been less sensitive if the constitutionality of the statute as applied to a married couple had been the issue before it. Moreover, the case would almost surely have come out the other way given the language of the opinion in *Griswold v. Connecticut*. Georgia in fact acknowledged that the statute would have been unconstitutional if applied to a married couple.

But is the principle that supports Hardwick's claim, which is an application of the "liberty interest" that supports a woman's claim to an abortion, basically different from the claim of a married couple? Such a couple would have the additional argument drawn from the specific application of the principle in *Griswold.* Did Hardwick need that additional argument?

The Court stated—misstated, I believe—the principle at stake in *Roe v. Wade:* "The Due Process Clause of the Fourteenth Amendment . . . confer[s] a fundamental individual right to decide whether or not to beget or bear a child." This formulation foreclosed Hardwick's claim; indeed it would greatly dim the chances of a married couple. The Court did not take responsibility for this description of the principle set forth in *Roe.* It relied on a prior decision.

In *Carey v. Population Services International* (1976) a New York statute regulating the sale and advertising of contraceptives was held unconstitutional.[20] In the course of the opinion the Court did describe the principle established in *Roe v. Wade* in words similar to those quoted above. But in the context of *Carey* this should be read as a limited formulation of a larger principle, a formulation sufficient to resolve the case then before the Court.

The "right to decide whether or not to beget or bear a child" rests on the more general, qualified right of a woman to decide what happens in or to her body. This more general right, or principle, is the basis of Hardwick's claim. To defeat this claim by describing the principle in terms of a set of applications that have already been decided is not to be true to the process of adjudication. It is to fail to treat like cases alike. And the cases—*Roe v. Wade* and *Bowers v. Hardwick*—are alike to the extent that they rest on the same principle, as they should be seen to do.

But the principle may weigh differently in the two cases. I have argued that public morality is an appropriate source of law for a court in elaborating "liberty" in the due process clause of the Fourteenth Amendment. If *Bowers v. Hardwick* had been before the Court prior to its decision in *Griswold,* Hardwick could not have succeeded. It is indeed far from clear that he could have made out his case when he brought it by an appeal to public morality if he had been forced to limit judicial consideration to the rights of homosexuals. This was the Court's approach. It was the wrong approach, for here too the Court was not true to the process of adjudication.

Start instead with a married couple. *Griswold* controls. The public values that support that decision were strengthened by it. We can find a good deal of evidence for this in the hearings on the confirmation of Robert H. Bork for a seat on the Supreme Court. President Reagan nominated Bork to fill the vacancy created when Justice Lewis F. Powell, Jr., retired in 1987. The Senate turned Bork down, at least in part because he had publicly disagreed with the result in *Griswold*. Indeed the hearings suggest strong political approval of the principle advanced in *Griswold*, if not the weight of the principle.

Griswold involved only a state ban on the use of contraceptive devices by a married couple. Subsequent decisions, including *Carey,* invalidated state regulation of the sale of contraceptives to single persons. This evolving law reflected changing social attitudes toward sexual behavior, and perhaps influenced them. It seems reasonable to think that the evolution from *Griswold* to *Carey* would be repeated if a sodomy statute were held unconstitutional when applied to a married couple. Its application to an unmarried, heterosexual couple would probably be held unconstitutional. I say "probably" because I think the ruling would hinge at least in part on how much weight the Court gave to the many legislative judgments that sodomy is immoral, and, on the other side of the balance, to the lax enforcement of these statutes where the "crime" is performed in private.

This last point needs to be considered against the background of another case, *Stanley v. Georgia* (1969), "where the Court held that the First Amendment prevents conviction for possessing and reading obscene material in the privacy of [the] home."[21] For if liberty of expression has greater protection in one's home, why not other forms of liberty? Surely the answer, if there is one, can not turn on the text of the First Amendment, for it makes no distinction between activities performed in public and those performed in private.

At any rate, I suspect that the Court too was unsure about the constitutionality of the statute as applied to an unmarried heterosexual couple. This suggests that it should never have heard the case.

It did not have to: the case came from a court of appeals to the justices on a petition for certiorari (a formal request, made by the party who lost in the lower court, for review), and the Court did not have to grant the petition. (It generally takes four justices to grant certiorari, and it is done or not without oral argument). Nor did the Court have to explain itself if it denied the petition. Today almost all the Supreme Court's appellate jurisdiction is on petition for certiorari. It is almost all a discretionary jurisdiction. This means that on most occasions the justices decide what to decide, and, so long as there is a case, when to decide it. When the central constitutional issue rests on the interpretation of public values, judicial ambivalence counsels judicial restraint. And judicial restraint is best achieved by deciding not to decide. But the Court took the case, and once it had taken it the process of adjudication required that all the substantive issues I have adumbrated needed to be thought through before the weight of the principle that a person has the right to decide what happens in and to her or his body could properly be determined in the context of homosexual sodomy. This is part of the obligation of treating like cases alike. For if the conclusion were that heterosexual sodomy performed in private between unmarried consenting adults could not be criminalized, it would be difficult to make sodomy a crime for homosexuals. Indeed, it would be possible only if the Court determined that it was permissible under the equal protection clause for a legislature to draw distinctions in a criminal statute that turned on nothing but raw prejudice. For while AIDS is more prevalent among male homosexuals than among heterosexuals, surely there are less drastic ways to prevent its spread than by criminalizing for one group what is (hypothetically) legal for the other group.

Thinking through these issues is the central point of what Professor Wechsler referred to in his Holmes Lecture, perhaps unfortunately, as neutral principles (see chapter 2). As I see it, it is an aspect of the process of adjudication, a process that includes interpreting many sources of law, including public morality, as they come to bear on the meaning of constitutional text.

I have tried to do some interpreting of public morality at a substantive level, first with *Griswold* and then with abortion. And I have tried to undertake this interpretive enterprise while taking account of the unique environment that is the province of appellate adjudication.

PART IV

The Politics of the Indigestible

CHAPTER SEVEN

Judicial Mistake

The common-law method of constitutional adjudication that we have been examining better explains the Supreme Court's role in American government than either originalism or Justice Stone's footnote in *Carolene Products* does. Normatively it has the advantage of building change into law, change that takes into account contemporary substantive values as well as participational values.

An additional strength of the common-law method is its experiential familiarity: it is how courts generally adjudicate (or, more accurately, it is related to how they adjudicate). And as a method, it has some of the controls that exist in statutory interpretation, where the joint enterprise of ordering the future wisely is a cooperative undertaking between legislature and court. In constitutional adjudication, at least in those areas where public morality is the major source of law, judicial deference to the legislature serves a similar function where deference is due. But the relative finality of the Supreme Court's constitutional holdings, as contrasted with statutory holdings, raises the stakes. What is the constitutional substitute for legislative statutory revision? In thinking about this, recall that statutory revision, where it is possible, is itself problematic because legislatures are too busy to give regular review to decisional law and because it may be difficult to overturn statutory interpretation even when it is contrary to legislative purpose. This is often so where decisional law generates widespread public support.

One substitute for legislative revision is of course formal constitutional amendment. Under Article V of the Constitution (which also provides for the calling of a convention) two-thirds of both Houses of Congress may propose amendments to the Constitution. But the process is extraordinarily difficult: for an amendment to be adopted, three-fourths of the states must give their consent as well.

The Constitution has been amended only four times to overturn a Supreme Court decision. The Eleventh Amendment was adopted in response to the Court's holding in *Chisholm v. Georgia* that a state could be sued in federal court by a plaintiff from a different state.[1]

Constitutional amendments (and the Civil War) reversed the Supreme Court's *Dred Scott* decision, which upset the Missouri Compromise by ruling in effect that blacks were not citizens protected by the Constitution.[2] The Thirteenth Amendment ended slavery as an institution, and subsequent amendments guaranteed particular rights for blacks. But as we all know, the implementation of these rights has been and remains an exceedingly slow process.

The Sixteenth Amendment was adopted to change the results of *Pollock v. Farmer's Loan and Trust Co.,* in which a federal income tax was struck down.[3]

The Twenty-sixth Amendment overturned the Court's ruling in *Oregon v. Mitchell* that a federal law lowering the minimum voting age in state elections to eighteen was unconstitutional.[4]

It should be added that some proposed amendments have been of a structural sort: these have been aimed at affecting Court decisions indirectly by placing curbs on the Court rather than by attempting to overturn specific decisions. They have included unsuccessful efforts to subject the Court's decisions to another governmental tribunal, to require more than a majority of justices to strike down a law, to submit the Court's decisions to popular referenda, and to allow Congress to reenact laws held unconstitutional by the Court.

Given that only four Supreme Court decisions have been reversed by constitutional amendment even though there have been many unpopular decisions, it would seem that Article V is not an effective means of changing unpopular Court decisions. Success in its use requires that an extraordinary combination of social, economic, and political forces combine to achieve super majorities in multiple forums. Indeed, efforts to overturn especially controversial decisions are the least likely to clear the hurdles of Article V. But Professor Bruce Ackerman, in a number of lucid and provocative articles, has urged his readers to think of a political event that transforms the nation—the New Deal, for example—as the equivalent of a constitutional amendment authorized by "We the People," as he puts it.[5] Under this view, which Ackerman constructs from a close reading of American political history, there are additional methods available for amending the Constitution. Accordingly, the "constitutional amendment" plays a more important role in checking judicial power—as well as in explaining the exercise of judicial power—than is normally ascribed to it.

Judicial power is itself lodged in Article III, which after setting forth the Supreme Court's original jurisdiction, authorizes a grant of appellate jurisdiction as to law and fact, "with such Exceptions and under such Regulations as the Congress shall make." Students of Article III disagree about the extent to which this "exceptions clause" permits "jurisdiction stripping." But Congress does have substantial power to take jurisdiction away from the Court. It is however a power that has been exercised sparingly.

Congress had success with the exceptions clause in 1869, when it undertook to limit the Court's application of a reconstruction statute. In *Ex parte McCardle*, a southern newspaper editor held in military custody appealed from a denial of habeas corpus by challenging the constitutionality of the Military Reconstruction Act. Oral argument was heard before the Supreme Court, and Congress, fearing a threat to its reconstruction program, enacted a law repealing an earlier statute that had granted the Court jurisdiction to review circuit court denials of habeas corpus petitions. The Court promptly dismissed the editor's appeal, reasoning that "jurisdiction is the power to declare the law, and when it ceases to exist, the only function remaining to the courts is that of announcing the fact and dismissing the cause."[6]

While proposals to strip the Court of its jurisdiction have recently been introduced as legislation in a number of areas—school prayer cases, reapportionment, and abortion are examples—all have failed in Congress. In any event jurisdiction stripping does not eliminate the constitutional decision deemed offensive by the strippers. Earlier Supreme Court decisions remain authoritative to the extent that Supreme Court decisions are authoritative. Stripping removes the power of the Supreme Court to review decisions of lower courts. This means that the Court is denied the authority to police decisional conformity with its prior holdings.

Congressional restraint means that judicial review of the scope of the exceptions clause has been limited. Historically, congressional control of the Supreme Court's appellate jurisdiction has been little more than a political threat. But it is widely recognized that Congress does have broad control over lower federal courts. While there is disagreement about how extensive its power is, we do know that among other things Congress can restrict the remedies a court may impose, at least in some situations.For example, federal courts have limited authority to issue injunctions in labor disputes, and to some extent Congress can specify the court in which a case may be heard. Sometimes this power can sharply reduce the impact of a constitutional decision. Thus the bar on labor injunctions enacted in 1932 mitigated the effect on organized labor of Court rulings from the time of *Lochner* that protective labor legislation was unconstitutional.[7]

————

These formal controls, and others, such as control over the judiciary's budget, including control over judges' salary increases, would, if used, affect the development of law in different and perhaps unpredictable ways. According to one's view of adjudication, some of these controls are plainly wrongheaded ways to cabin the judiciary. Here there is room for substantial disagreement. It is clear, however, that in practice the controls are not comparable to the legislative power of statutory revision. Therefore if one is concerned about controlling the judiciary—and at one time or another most organized interest groups are—the search must be elsewhere. Please remember that the issue is not only democracy, at least not as it is practiced in the United States; it is finality.

Let me then make this claim: the substitutes in constitutional adjudication for statutory revision are separation of powers (in a nontechnical sense) and the American people (in perhaps more than a metaphorical sense). To unpack this claim it may be helpful to start with a bicentennial political document.

In a lecture delivered in the fall of 1986 at Tulane University, Edwin Meese III, then the attorney general of the United States, drew a sharp distinction between the Constitution and constitutional law. He quoted the legal historian Charles Warren to the effect that "however the Court may interpret the provisions of the Constitution, it is still the Constitution which is the law, not the decisions of the Court." Meese continued: "By this, of course, Charles Warren did not mean that a constitutional decision by the Supreme Court lacks the character of law. Obviously it does have binding quality: It binds the parties in a case and also the executive branch for whatever enforcement is necessary. But such a decision does not establish a 'supreme law of the land' that is binding on all persons and parts of government, henceforth and forevermore."[8]

"Henceforth and forevermore" is a long time. But how about until the Court overrules itself or there is that extraordinary constitutional amendment overruling the Court? This is not Meese's vision of the role of the judiciary in American government. It is, however, the Court's view—or at least it has so advised the nation. In a dictum in the desegregation case *Cooper v. Aaron* (1958), the Court made it clear to state officials in Arkansas who were resisting the integration of a high school in Little Rock that they were bound by a prior Supreme Court decision, by constitutional law (namely the holding in *Brown v. Board of Education*), and not by the officials' different interpretation of the Constitution. Put another and by now familiar way, *Brown* did not merely resolve a dispute; it regulated the future of those who were not parties in the adjudication.

The Court stated it this way:

> [W]e should answer the premise of the actions of the Governor and Legislature that they are not bound by our holding in the Brown case. It is necessary only to recall some basic constitutional propositions which are settled doctrine. Article VI of the Constitution makes the Constitution the "supreme Law of the Land." In 1803, Chief Justice Marshall, speaking for a unanimous Court, referring to the Constitution as "the fundamental and paramount law of the nation," declared in the notable case of Marbury v. Madison . . . , that "It is emphatically the province and duty of the judicial department to say what the law is." This decision declared the basic principle that the federal judiciary is supreme in the exposition of the law of the Constitution, and that principle has ever since been respected by this Court and the Country as a permanent and indispensable feature of our constitutional system. It follows that the interpretation of the Fourteenth Amendment enunciated by this Court in the Brown case is the supreme law of the land, and Art. VI of the Constitution makes it of binding effect on the States "any Thing in the Constitution or Laws of any State to the Contrary notwithstanding." Every state legislator and executive and judicial officer is solemnly committed by oath taken pursuant to Art. VI, Para. 3, "to support this Constitution."[9]

As Professor Gerald Gunther of Stanford University has pointed out, it is not clear that *Cooper v. Aaron* is merely following *Marbury v. Madison*, as the Court seems to imply. *Cooper* insists on "judicial exclusiveness" in constitutional interpretation, *Marbury* only on "judicial authority to interpret the Constitution."[10] This distinction is of course extraordinarily important. In one way or another, many presidents have accepted judicial authority and rejected judicial exclusiveness. None did it with a clearer understanding of the structure of adjudication and the American system than Abraham Lincoln. He separated the resolution of disputes (once done, surely exclusive) from regulation, a powerful and potentially final method of ordering the future when large constitutional issues are at stake. And with respect to such regulation, he rejected judicial exclusiveness. Here is what Lincoln said on this matter in his First Inaugural Address, on March 4, 1861:

> I do not forget the position assumed by some that constitutional questions are to be decided by the Supreme Court, nor do I deny that such decisions must be binding in any case upon the parties to a suit as to the object of that suit, while they are also entitled to very high respect and consideration in all parallel cases by all other departments of the Government. And while it is obviously possible that such decision may be erroneous in any given case, still the evil effect following it, being limited to that particular case, with the chance that it may be overruled and never become a precedent for other cases, can better be borne than could the evils of a different practice. At the same time, the candid citizen must confess that if the policy of the Government upon vital questions affecting the whole people is to be irrevocably fixed by decisions of the Supreme Court, the instant they are made in ordinary litigation between parties in personal actions, the people will have ceased to be their own rulers, having to that extent practically resigned their Government into the hands of that eminent tribunal.

Meese is no Lincoln, and he doesn't get it quite right when he insists that "the necessary distinction [is] between the Constitution and constitutional law." While this distinction is an acceptable shorthand if it is not taken too seriously, there is every reason to assume that Meese was very serious indeed. The former attorney general is an adherent of originalism, and true belief in the separation between the Constitution and constitutional law is consistent with at least some versions of that flawed doctrine. But separation cannot be rigorously maintained. The Constitution is a two-hundred-year-old text that has been interpreted and reinterpreted by people in numerous roles: critics, advisors, and participants in institutional decisionmaking. Try as one might, one cannot recover the pristine or preinterpreted Constitution. It exists only as parchment.

But what are we to say about the authoritativeness of the Supreme Court's constitutional interpretations? Should we side with the Court's dictum in *Cooper v. Aaron* or with Abraham Lincoln? And should it matter that the Court was defending its antisegregation decision while Lincoln articulated his position as part of an attack on the Court's holding in favor of slavery in *Dred Scott?* These questions raise large issues requiring a framework for discussion. One framework is suggested by the process of constitutional adjudication as we have observed it (lawyers arguing to win, judges negotiating to achieve a majority decision) and from the sources of law used by the participants in that process—for example history, precedent, and public morality. The disagreement that exists over the persuasiveness of the decisions rendered by the Supreme Court, coupled with the impossibility in many situations of effecting legislative revision, makes it appropriate sometimes for the Court itself to change its prior rulings. And as Lincoln seems to have suggested, sometimes it is also appropriate for others to work for judicial revision. A major first question then—a question that I examined glancingly in the last chapter—is when. Put this question a little bit differently: how should the Court get information to decide whether it should overrule its prior decision, and what kind of information does it need? One thing the Court might like to know initially is whether its prior decision was, to use Lincoln's word, "erroneous." So let's begin by trying to develop a conception of judicial mistake.

I am interested in two types of judicial mistake. Each is related to a type of justification that a court might offer for a decision. And it is this relationship that connects the topic of judicial mistake with that of the sources of law. Courts—at least appellate courts—generally believe themselves obligated to justify their holdings. There are many standard modes of justification: an appeal to a legislative command, to a judicial precedent, to history, to an analogous development in another jurisdiction or in a related area of law. Moreover, the consequences that will attend a decision can serve as its justification; so can an appeal to public values.

My interest is with these latter two types of justification. The first, or consequentialist, justification, explicitly looks to the future. The claim is that the holding and others that follow it will change the behavior of individuals or institutions. The line of decision serves a policy, it effectuates a societal goal; the justification is in terms of benefits and costs.

The second type of justification in a sense looks to the past. It is not couched in what will be or in a goal toward which we are moving. The holding has persuasiveness because it vindicates public values by articulating a principle connected to these values; the justification is made in terms of rights and obligations.

I am not saying that a decision justified by an appeal to public values does not have significant consequences. It does. *Roe v. Wade* is clear proof of this. And as I suggested in chapter 6, some of these consequences constitute an important reason for not overruling *Roe* even if a majority of the Court now believes that *Roe* was to at least some extent a mistake (as *Webster* suggests they do believe). Nor am I contradicting my frequently made claim that regulation, as contrasted with the resolution of disputes, is almost always the principal reason for constitutional adjudication in the Supreme Court. But there is more than one way to justify a piece of regulation, and my point is that in this class of cases the Court has not undertaken to justify the initial decision by the consequences that will flow from that decision.

An analogy may help. Assume a statute so clear that for a given set of facts we can get away with saying that there are no questions of interpretation. When a court applies the statute, it will rest its opinion on the plain meaning of the statute and the authority of the legislature to enact it. That authority and the statute's plain meaning are the justification for a decision that has consequences; the consequences, however, are not the justification for the decision. In *Roe* public values are the source of the Court's authority. They are the source of law used to elaborate "liberty" in the due process clause. They serve as the justification for the decision. That decision has had enormous consequences for American society in general and women in particular.

The two types of justification I am interested in are hard to discover in pure form. Courts understandably tend to mix them together. Still, one justification or the other may dominate a decision. And in trying to understand judicial mistake, it behooves us to try to draw the distinction.

Consider the following examples. First policy. The decision in *New York Times v. Sullivan* is justified in consequentialist terms.[11] The case held that absent actual malice, the First Amendment, incorporated into the Fourteenth Amendment and thereby applied to the states, bars them from awarding damages to public officials for false and defamatory statements relating to their official conduct. At its most abstract, the goal to be fostered through this holding is the sound working of American democracy; somewhat less abstractly, the goal is "a commitment . . . that debate on public issues should be uninhibited, robust, and wide-open." The Court's justification took this form: without the holding, "critics of official conduct may be deterred from voicing their criticism, even though it is believed to be true and even though it is in fact true because of doubt whether it can be proved in court or fear of having to do so." The common law of defamation, the Court reasoned, "dampens the vigor and limits the variety of public debate." In short, the decision was justified by predictable consequences that serve a desirable goal.

Contrast this with the dissent in *Olmstead v. United States* (1928) of Justice Louis D. Brandeis, a member of the Court from 1916 to 1939. At issue in that famous case was whether wiretapping by federal officers constituted an unreasonable search and seizure under the Fourth Amendment. Listen to Brandeis:

> The makers of our Constitution undertook to secure conditions favorable to the pursuit of happiness. They recognized the significance of man's spiritual nature, of his feelings and of his intellect. They knew that only a part of the pain, pleasure and satisfactions of life are to be found in material things. They sought to protect Americans in their beliefs, their thoughts, their emotions and their sensations. They conferred, as against the government, the right to be let alone—the most comprehensive of rights and the right most valued by civilized men. To protect that right, every unjustifiable intrusion by the government upon the privacy of the individual, whatever the means employed, must be deemed a violation of the fourth Amendment.[12]

Now of course, if Brandeis is "doing" history he sounds like an originalist. He is attributing a great deal to the "makers of our Constitution," given that he is concerned with a contemporary technology in a strange world. But he is not performing as a historian in any conventional sense. His is a quest for the wellsprings of our public morality.

I know one might argue that the holding urged by Brandeis in *Olmstead* is justified by him in much the same way the *Sullivan* rule is justified: in consequentialist or policy terms. But to follow this line of reasoning would be mistaken. It would show either an insensitivity to linguistic nuance or a determination to conflate concepts that it is useful although difficult to keep separate. In *Sullivan* the justification for a decision protecting expression is the timid behavior of critics of the government who are faced with the common law of defamation. In *Olmstead* Brandeis is not concerned directly or principally with the behavior of government officials who authorize wiretapping; his concern is with the individual's right to be let alone. The decision that he would have had the Court adopt did not depend for its validity on the subsequent conduct of the officials; less wiretapping was desirable, but the justification for the proposed decision was individual privacy. That right was what Brandeis wished the Court to vindicate. In contrast, *Sullivan* rests on a prediction about how potential critics of government will conduct themselves when they are released from the fear of litigation: an increase in "the vigor and variety of public debate" not only is desirable, it is the justification for the rule. The right of the individual to speak—to exercise autonomy—is a welcome side effect.

This distinction between two types of justification for constitutional decisions suggests in turn a distinction between two types of judicial mistake. If it became clear that *New York Times v. Sullivan* did not have the consequences the Court predicted, that the behavior of potential critics of government did not change, and that "the vigor and variety of public debate" had not been altered by the decision, then *New York Times v. Sullivan* would be either a constitutional mistake or at least a decision in quest of a new justification.

The distinguished jurist Benjamin N. Cardozo, who served on the Supreme Court from 1932 to 1938 after a long career on the New York Court of Appeals, spoke in a different context about common-law cases: "Those that cannot prove their worth and strength by the test of experience, are sacrificed mercilessly and thrown into the void."[13]

I would not think this was proper if there were independent reasons for sticking to precedent, and there is good reason to believe that Cardozo did not think so either. But put that to one side for now and assume, in a particular case, that the policies that explain stare decisis are insufficient to support an adherence to precedent. How should we interpret Cardozo's "test of experience"? What does it mean? The answer, I suppose, lies in social science investigation: empirical research based on a statistically valid methodology. In addition to *New York Times v. Sullivan*, consider some other candidates, hypothetical and real, for this "test of experience": a constitutional decision to exclude the introduction in criminal trials of illegally obtained evidence because of the presumed deterrent effect that this exclusion has on police behavior; a constitutional decision rejecting juries of fewer than twelve members because of the presumably decreased protection that the defendant has when the jury is smaller; a determination that the death penalty is unconstitutional in felony murder cases because it fails to deter felony murder.

Without in any way implying criticism of the social sciences, I think we know that even if they were possible, scientific tests of experience would fall short of clear conclusions in at least some of these situations, or in others we could think of.[14] Nor are we apt to get better results from any other "test of experience," such as informed intuition.

This conclusion about the lack of clear conclusions gives me pause about the enthusiastic use of consequentialist or policy justifications in constitutional law. This use seems acceptable enough if the evidence on which the policy is based is clear. This may be the situation some of the time. When it is not, when judges rely on intuition but not knowledge and social scientists or other data collectors cannot tell them very much about the consequences of legal rules, should not policy be the domain of the legislatures? Should it not be subject to the trade-offs of elective politics? And generally, should judicial inquiry into the policy aspects of such decisions not be restrained?

If this problem is viewed through the lens of judicial mistake, with only a weak presumption in favor of stare decisis, a judicial declaration of unconstitutionality should prove difficult to reverse because of the difficulty of disproving its empirical assumptions. And unless the societal goals that the policy serves have changed, this is the only proper reason for overruling the decision. Public or political reaction, for example, is not evidence that the exclusionary rule is wrong if the exclusionary rule deters illegal searches and seizures and if deterrence is the reason for the rule.

This suggests that while forward-looking justifications for constitutional decisions may appear to respond to the regulatory aspects of adjudication, such justifications can sometimes be troublesome:

either they may have more finality than is healthy for a constitutional solution based on problematic assumptions, or they may tend not to endure for reasons that are at best difficult to explain.

Two caveats. First, the exclusionary rule as judicial policy is substantially less troublesome than defamation and the First Amendment, because it redirects governmental activity without changing the government's goal (as I have noted earlier). In this sense it is far less final than *Sullivan*, which substantially restricts the government's protection of reputation. Second, while what I have said should be taken as requiring a justification and not a rationalization for a constitutional rule, it should not be taken as a criticism of the holding in *New York Times v. Sullivan*, or the exclusionary rule cases, or any other substantive constitutional holding. It questions only the Court's justification. Thus the exclusionary rule could perhaps be justified in Brandeisian terms as an aspect of "the privacy of the individual," without regard to its effect on police practices.

Let me turn now to a second type of judicial mistake, one associated with decisions that are justified in terms of public values. As I have suggested, it is not difficult to imagine that public values are sometimes less than scrupulously regarded in the give and take of the legislative process, with its necessary compromises, trade-offs, and essential goal orientation. Nor should it be surprising that mistakes occur in the judicial process. In the interactive process of deciding on grounds of public values, even the most conscientious judge can get these values or their weights wrong.

But what is the criterion here for judicial mistake? What is the meaning of Cardozo's "test of experience" in this context? It cannot be based on an empirical investigation, or at least I do not think it can. Perhaps it can be the community's reaction to a judicial decision. When the Justices get public values wrong in constitutional cases, they hear about it. Of course, it is also true that when they get them right they hear about it. In both situations there may be turmoil, resistance, and threats from other governmental entities, from private groups, institutions, and individuals. There is always discussion and analysis; some of it may even be informed and dispassionate.

Put it all together, and when considered along with what the Court has said it may constitute a rich political dialogue, one that may give the Court the information it needs if it is to know whether it has made a mistake.

CHAPTER EIGHT

The Authoritativeness of the Court's Constitutional Interpretation

The rich political dialogue that sometimes follows a Supreme Court decision takes many forms and invites us to make some distinctions. If accepted, this invitation will take us back to Attorney General Meese and President Lincoln, and into the role of citizens and groups in our political culture.

One broad and probably necessary distinction is between government officials and private citizens. Edwin Meese and the Supreme Court in *Cooper v. Aaron* were disagreeing about the obligation of officials to consider themselves bound by the Supreme Court's interpretation of the Constitution. Like Lincoln, however, Meese should not be understood to have suggested that the Court's holding in a case did not control the outcome of that case: all officials, he agreed, were under an obligation to respect the aspects of the Court's actions that resolved the dispute at hand, and to give effect to these aspects if they were called on to do so. The disagreement is over interpretation as binding regulation in a case where the official disagrees strongly with the Court's constitutional interpretation, where the official believes that the Court has made a mistake.

Government officials—federal and state—are under an obligation to support the Constitution. When they act in their official capacity they are bound by oath to conform that action to the constraints mandated by the Constitution. And so, at a very general level, the question is what an official who interprets the Constitution differently from the Court should do.

Certainly *Cooper v. Aaron* is a plausible gloss on *Marbury v. Madison*: The Constitution is law and the judicial department is peculiarly well suited to say what the law is. Once it has spoken, that's that: other officials are under an obligation to recognize that they must obey.

But this argument begs the question; it assumes that the Supreme Court's interpretation is in effect supreme law. It assumes that we have a rule recognizing this, a bright, clear, or clean "rule of recognition," lodged either in the text of the Constitution or in constitutional practice, making the Court's interpretation final and binding regulation. But the text does not answer the question: "This Constitution," Article VI reads, "shall be the supreme Law of the Land." The text is silent about the authoritativeness of the Court's interpretation of "this Constitution." Nor does practice provide a bright rule of recognition. Most of the time the Court's contested interpretations are accepted as regulation; there may be kicking and screaming by some, but the gauntlet of resistance is not thrown down.

Consider the Court's relatively recent adventures with the constitutionality of federal minimum wage legislation when applied to employees of state and local government. The decision in *National League of Cities v. Usery* (1976) had denied Congress the power to set a minimum wage for city employees.[1] This decision, overruling the case of *Maryland v. Wirtz*,[2] was enthusiastically received by most municipal and state officials, for it gave them more authority and flexibility over local budgets. Nine years later the Court held in *Garcia v. San Antonio Transit Authority* that *Usery* had been a mistake.[3] *Garcia* overruled *Usery*. In it the Court concluded that the earlier Court (or the Court earlier) had misunderstood the reach of congressional power under the commerce clause and the constraint imposed by the Tenth Amendment ("The powers not delegated to the United States by the Constitution, nor prohibited by it to the States, are reserved to the States respectively, or to the people"). Parenthetically, *Garcia* is like *Goldman v. Weinberger* in that Congress can change its regulatory effect by changing the statute that the Court held constitutional.

State and municipal officials were very upset by *Garcia*, thought it wrong, and have tried in a variety of ways to reverse it. But they did not attack the authority of the decision as regulation. And given judicial review, and the justifications for it that we have examined, this must be the standard response of the government official. First, without this response, and since the Constitution is a form of law, it would be difficult or even impossible to achieve the stability needed to make a complex system work, especially a federal system. Second, the Supreme Court adjudicates disputes, but it is the regulatory effect of its adjudication that is the Court's reason for being. Because other courts decide first, the Supreme Court is not needed to resolve a particular dispute, although a particular dispute is necessary to the jurisdiction of the Court under Article III of the Constitution.

But the standard response of accepting the Court's regulation is not the only response. Our practice has another side that shows itself from time to time and has found expression in the strong words of great political figures. In the last chapter we heard from Lincoln. Here is Jefferson, in a letter to Abigail Adams written in 1804:

> You seem to think it devolved on the judges to decide on the validity of the sedition law. But nothing in the Constitution has given them a right to decide for the Executive, more than to the Executive to decide for them. Both magistracies are equally independent in the sphere of action assigned to them. The judges, believing the law constitutional, had a right to pass a sentence of fine and imprisonment; because that power was placed in their hands by the Constitution. But the Executive, believing the law to be unconstitutional, was bound to remit the execution of it; because that power has been confided to him by the Constitution. That instrument meant that its co-ordinate branches should be checks on each other. But the opinion which gives to the judges the right to decide what laws are constitutional, and what not, not only for themselves in their own sphere of action, but for the Legislature & Executive also, in their spheres, would make the judiciary a despotic branch.[4]

And here is Lincoln again, this time from the great Senate campaign debates with Stephen Douglas:

> I have expressed heretofore, and I now repeat, my opposition to the Dred Scott Decision but I should be allowed to state the nature of that opposition. . . . . I do not resist it. If I wanted to take Dred Scott from his master, I would be interfering with property. [But] I am doing no such thing as that, but all that I am doing is refusing to obey it as a political rule. If I were in Congress, and a vote should come up on a question whether slavery should be prohibited in a new territory, in spite of that Dred Scott decision, I would vote that it should.
>
> We oppose the Dred Scott decision in a certain way. [We] do not propose that when Dred Scott has been decided to be a slave by the court, we, as a mob, will decide him to be free. We do not propose that, when any other one, or one thousand, shall be decided by that court to be slaves, we will in any violent way disturb the rights of property thus settled; but we nevertheless do oppose that decision as a political rule which shall be binding on the voter, to vote for nobody who thinks it wrong, which shall be binding on the members of Congress or the President to favor no measure that does not actually concur with the principles of that decision. [We] propose so resisting it as to have it reversed if we can, and a new judicial rule established upon this subject.[5]

The practice of official disagreement may take many forms besides letters, addresses, and debates. But in the first place, let's put to one side the situation where an official feels capable in good faith of distinguishing a statute, for example, from the regulation created by a prior Court decision. This may be done by interpreting that decision in a good, lawyerly fashion. Consider the following from Andrew Jackson's veto message, delivered in 1832, of a statute providing for a national bank. An earlier statute establishing such a bank had been held constitutional. In the famous case of *McCulloch v. Maryland* (1819), the Court relied in part on the nature of the bank as a "necessary and proper" adjunct to the functioning of federal governmental policy.[6] Jackson wrote:

> [Under] the decision of the Supreme Court [it] is the exclusive province of Congress and the President to decide whether the particular features of this act are necessary and proper in order to enable the bank to perform conveniently and efficiently the public duties assigned to it as a fiscal agent, and therefore constitutional, or unnecessary and improper, and therefore unconstitutional. Without commenting on the general principle affirmed by the Supreme Court, let us examine the details of this act in accordance with the rule of legislative action which they have laid down. It will be found that many of the powers and privileges conferred on it can not be supposed necessary for the purpose for which it is proposed to be created, and are not, therefore, means necessary to attain the end in view, and consequently not justified by the Constitution.

President Jackson was suggesting that while a national bank might have been constitutional earlier since Congress and the president decided it was "necessary and proper" to the functioning of the federal government, he did not believe that the legislation placed before him for his constitutional decision was necessary and proper. He read *McCulloch* as empowering him to make an independent determination of that question.

But even if a prior Supreme Court decision cannot be read in such an empowering way, isn't it perfectly proper for a president to exercise the veto and rest its exercise on constitutional grounds? The president is operating in the executive realm. There is no judicial review of the executive action. Is it not appropriate for the president to join issue with the Court over their disagreement? This was President Jackson's position—indeed he went beyond it—in another portion of his bank veto message:

> It is maintained by the advocates of the bank that its constitutionality in all its features ought to be considered as settled by

precedent and by the decision of the Supreme Court. To this conclusion I cannot assent. Mere precedent is a dangerous source of authority, and should not be regarded as deciding questions of constitutional power except where the acquiescence of the people and the States can be considered as well settled. [If] the opinion of the Supreme Court covered the whole ground of this act, it ought not to control the coordinate authorities of this Government. The Congress, the Executive, and the Court must each for itself be guided by its own opinion of the Constitution. Each public officer who takes an oath to support the Constitution swears that he will support it as he understands it, and not as it is understood by others. It is as much the duty of the House of Representatives, of the Senate, and of the President to decide upon the constitutionality of any bill or resolution which may be presented to them for passage or approval as it is of the supreme judges when it may be brought before them for judicial decision. The opinion of the judges has no more authority over Congress than the opinion of Congress has over the judges, and on that point the President is independent of both. The authority of the Supreme Court must not, therefore, be permitted to control the Congress or the Executive when acting in their legislative capacities, but to have only such influence as the force of their reasoning may deserve.

But does this also mean that where the president favors a statute but believes it is unconstitutional even though it raises questions that are indistinguishable from other questions that the Court has held constitutional, the presidential oath of office requires a veto? While the case is not apt to arise—presidents are practical politicians—the answer is no. Presidents are free to recognize that they may be fallible; they too can defer. Their deference may result from the realization that they are not always under an obligation to interpret the Constitution because they have taken an oath to "preserve, protect and defend" it.

Suppose now that there has been no prior Supreme Court decision. The president favors the legislation but believes it is unconstitutional. Is there an obligation to veto it because of the presidential oath to protect the Constitution? The president cannot defer to a prior Court decision, but there is nothing wrong in deciding that it is prudent to leave the constitutional question to the courts. Alexander Bickel once wrote about the passive virtues, those exhibited by the Court when it decides not to decide if a decision on the constitutional merits is unwise for the nation. Some have thought this impermissible where the Court's jurisdiction is mandatory.[7] Whatever the answer to this question, now largely moot (today the Supreme Court's jurisdiction is almost entirely discretionary), the passive virtues must be available to a president, governor, or legislator. Surely then, in assessing constitutional responsibility, we can state the following as the minimum demanded by practical politics: it is permissible when prudent for partisan political actors to leave constitutional interpretation to the judicial department.

Please understand that while I may be disagreeing with some of the implications in President Jackson's veto message, I am not suggesting that practical politics justify violating one's constitutional oath. My claim is an interpretive one: leaving constitutional questions to the judicial branch can be consistent with supporting, preserving, protecting, or defending the Constitution, and therefore with the oath taken by a legislator or executive. While others may disagree, it seems to me that this is an easy case.

It is easy, too, to state the obligation of federal and state judges who disagree with Supreme Court interpretation. Here there is no separation of powers, no argument for horizontal authority or in some situations for equal authority. Here hierarchy is the nature of governance and it demands that the Supreme Court's interpretation of the Constitution be followed as regulation or, to use Lincoln's term, as the "political rule." The judge who thinks the Court is mistaken must try hard to distinguish prior cases, but if it is not possible to do this in good faith the judge must either follow the Court (if conscience permits) or resign.

Lincoln's case is much harder. There a nonjudicial officer knows the scope of the Court's interpretation, believes strongly that it is mistaken, and is prepared openly to disregard it as regulation. While Lincoln's position on *Dred Scott* must be right no matter what (there are some things that are so evil they can neither be accepted nor dodged by resignation), and while there may be other situations where rejection by an official of a Supreme Court decision as a "political rule" is a felt political necessity, I want to suggest that such rejection can most easily be justified where the source of law that supports the decision is public morality and the official is strongly of the opinion that the Court has made a mistake.

This claim applies to state as well as federal officials, to governors and legislators as well as presidents and members of Congress. It must therefore rest on arguments that are different from some of those advanced by the presidents I have quoted. Some of what they said turned on the tripartite nature of the federal government, on the horizontal, equal division of authority, on the separation of federal powers among the executive, legislative, and judicial branches.

The basis for my claim rests at least in part on the nature of public morality. Remember that this is an interactive concept: it is neither found by the decisionmaker who uses it as a source of law nor created by the decisionmaker. Moreover, in adjudication it emerges through the distinctive process that we have been examining. It is a decisionmaking process that is very different from executive and legislative processes; and process shapes substance. How could it be otherwise when the evidence considered and the analysis employed are so powerfully influenced by institutional considerations?

Accordingly, in a sense we can say that the official who disagrees with a judicial interpretation of the Constitution based on public morality is claiming that the Court has made a mistake and is trying actively to persuade the country and the Court of this mistake.

I take it to be the function of all our government officials to try to respond to public values and at the same time necessarily to shape them, to press us to accept their understanding, to "read" public values in a way that accentuates what they in their institutional roles believe to be desirable for the country.

While federal judges are often better positioned than other public officials to perform this interpretive function—their role defines them as disinterested and the constitutional structure shields them from short-run political pressure—Supreme Court justices are fallible. This is why they should give some deference to the legislature and executive when public values have been addressed by these agencies before judicial review, and it is why public officials may claim some authority after such review. But given our general practice of accepting the authority of the Court's interpretation, and the need for stability that such a practice serves, serious challenges must be reserved for issues of profound moment—as they have been.

I shall return to this shortly, but now let's look at another process involving government officials that sometimes may be used either to reinforce or to undermine the Supreme Court's interpretation of the Constitution.

The interpretive battle for the meaning of the Constitution has many participants and takes many forms. One additional form involving government officials is the nomination of a Supreme Court justice and the confirmation process before the Senate.

Surely it is appropriate for the president to nominate a qualified person who shares the administration's perspectives on constitutional issues. Depending on the times, this shared perspective may emphasize reinforcing or undermining existing Court interpretations of the Constitution. But it is often not easy to forecast whether a potential nominee shares the administration's perspectives. Constitutional issues can shift dramatically.

Felix Frankfurter was a political liberal who believed in judicial self-restraint and deference in constitutional interpretation to the legislative branch. He brought to judging a strong presumption that statutes are constitutional. Statutes regulating the economy were the issue of the day when he was appointed in 1939. Did the commerce clause empower Congress to order labor relations? Did the due process clause permit it to set minimum wages? His answer about congressional power was an emphatic yes. It remained so when the issues shifted to whether Congress could substantially curb the political and civil rights of individuals in the name of national security.

The point is of course not whether FDR would have been disappointed with Justice Frankfurter's role in postwar America, but rather—contrary to the views of many—that judicial philosophy and not political ideology may govern constitutional interpretation, and that although the two are related in complex ways, they are not the same.

This conclusion probably means that in spite of all the rhetoric about the long-run impact of judicial appointments, an administration is apt to be preoccupied with forecasting a potential nominee's position on the present constitutional agenda. How successful the forecast will be depends on the transparency of the agenda and knowledge about a nominee's position. In the case of Robert Bork, there was both transparency and knowledge.

What about the Senate's role in this phase of the interpretative battle? The Constitution provides that the President "shall nominate, and by and with the advice and consent of the Senate shall appoint . . . Judges of the Supreme Court." There is disagreement over how the Senate should go about discharging its obligation to consent or not to consent. All would agree that it should do so with dignity. And probably all would agree that it should inquire into a nominee's intellectual and moral qualifications to sit at the top of the federal judiciary. But should the Senate focus on issues similar to those that the president addresses in making the nominating decision? Sometimes in the past it has done so; sometimes not. And although the Senate's approach and decision call for constitutional interpretation, they like many other approaches and situations are not subject to judicial review. In this technical sense and in many other senses as well, the Senate's approach and decision on a Supreme Court nomination are political questions.

What then should one advise the conscientious senator? The answer, I believe, is that each senator should focus on issues similar to those that a president properly addresses when making a nominating decision. The reason for this conclusion is simply that the regulatory aspect of Supreme Court decisions are subject to revision by the Court itself. As we have seen, the process of adjudication entails the refinement, extension or contraction, distinguishing or rejecting of prior constitutional interpretations.

Consider at least some of what this means. First, lawyers representing clients shape cases to achieve interpretations consistent with interests that their clients share with others similarly situated or likeminded. Second, such factions or interest groups press their interpretive position with a variety of other methods, including the lobbying of legislators to do what is possible. And what is possible may include legislation that restricts or eliminates the future effect of the Court's constitutional pronouncements, legislation that removes jurisdiction from the Court, and proposals for constitutional amendments. The failure of these legislative attempts is not unimportant in establishing the climate in which subsequent adjudication takes place. For unless Supreme Court justices were to see themselves as infallible, they would hear at least as background noise the views of other interpreters of the Constitution, including officials who oppose the regulatory aspects of Supreme Court decisions. As we shall see, the public forum is another place for this sort of noise: the learned and popular journals, the newspaper and television screen, and the political platform, parades, and rallies. Given the nature of public values, this noise is of interest where those values are a source of law.

One way of thinking about the art of advocacy, and ultimately of judging, is to recognize that background noise has in it good and bad interpretive arguments that must be distinguished along with reasons and rationalizations. Like the wheat and the chaff, they must be separated.

All this means that constitutional interpretation is a dynamic, complex process. Senate confirmation proceedings are a part of that process. Indeed they are especially vital. If properly conducted, the hearings should produce a lot of wheat and very little chaff. How important the hearings are should depend on what is known about a nominee's judicial philosophy, for how a potential Supreme Court justice views constitutional adjudication, and how that view articulates on the present constitutional agenda, can critically influence the Court. And as we know, the Court is the institution that not only has the authority to interpret the Constitution but that has an interpretive voice which, while not exclusive, is surely more influential than any other.

In sum, the appointment of a Supreme Court justice and the confirmation process before the Senate must take account of the following truth: the nature of constitutional interpretation in the process of adjudication inevitably means that constitutional law is shaped, influenced, indeed made by those authorized to interpret. This is not a dirty little secret. And neither is it an institutional failure demanding systemic reform.

We have seen that Supreme Court justices, while the most important, are not the only government officials authorized to interpret the Constitution. But what about the role of ordinary Americans, nonofficials? What is their role?

Start with the proposition that professionals have an obligation to interpret the Constitution. Professionals include, but are not limited to, lawyers—practicing as well as academic—and other students of the Constitution such as historians, political scientists, philosophers, and journalists. In a sense all are undertaking to shape the law through analysis.

No one would suggest, however, that the law professor (the critic) writing in a professional journal about the unconstitutionality of, let us say, the Georgia sodomy statute is making law in any way similar to that of the Supreme Court when it sustained the constitutionality of that statute in *Bowers v. Hardwick* (see chapter 6). Yet both law professor and Court are interpreting the Constitution, and the law professor's interpretation is not necessarily unimportant to a continuing discussion of the soundness of the Supreme Court's decision and to efforts of advocates to distinguish and undermine the decision in its regulatory aspect.

Moreover, the work of a scholarly critic is not the only or even the most important type of private activity that counts. Action calculated to produce legislation is a powerful method of law reform, of law creation, of law making. So too is action calculated to result in litigation. The first needs no special examination here. (Remember that the Court's constitutional interpretation may not be susceptible to legislative amendment.) The second does.

Recall the civil rights movement that followed *Brown*. One target of the heroic efforts to desegregate the South was discrimination that could plausibly be seen as private activity, although often it was private activity that was consistent with state law. An example of this would be the refusal of the owner of a lunch counter to serve blacks. If truly private, discrimination was not barred by the equal protection clause of the Fourteenth Amendment. And at the time, and before the Civil Rights Act of 1964, it was not thought that federal statutory law reached private discrimination—discrimination, that is, by individuals who are not government officials. Much litigation ensued over what was private and what was state action, over what constituted enough state involvement in an event to make the equal protection clause applicable. The line moved. To reduce discrimination, state action was found in situations where a generation earlier it probably would not have been.[8]

This was accomplished in the end by the process of adjudication. But if we focus on the primary activity that gave rise to the litigation perhaps we can make some interesting observations. First, distinguish between activity that is protected by the free speech provisions of the First and Fourteenth Amendments and other activity. To advocate the desegregation of a lunch counter is permissible. The advocates may claim that desegregation should happen because it is the right thing even if it is not constitutionally required. They may also claim that desegregation is constitutionally required—indeed they are likely to, whether state law requires segregated facilities or is silent about the matter. They would insist that all state law consistent with segregation is unconstitutional.

Second, action that entails more than speech—occupying another's property might be an example—may constitute the primary activity that results in litigation. That activity too may be justified in the two ways that advocacy can be justified (desegregation is the right thing; the constitutionally required thing). But here the activity may not be protected. Even if it is peaceful—and whether an occupation would be so characterized is not itself always so clear—it may be illegal. Whether it is may depend on whether the constitutional claims are ultimately vindicated. An interesting aspect of this is that the answer itself is influenced by the activity: professionally and skillfully advocating an outcome that turns on an interpretation of the Constitution may properly influence the judiciary in interpreting the Constitution. As we have seen from chapter 1 on, this is the way adjudication works.

There is another point to be made about private activity directed at precipitating litigation through action with the hope of shaping constitutional doctrine. As a society we must be tolerant of the competing views of various groups about constitutional meaning, particularly when we are trying to construct a public morality and regulate by adjudication. For a public morality must be as inclusive as possible and adjudication needs its substitutes for the access and accountability that theoretically exist where regulation is by legislation. This means that the political speech we hate must be vigorously defended and that the state must not be harsh in its response to peaceful civil disobedience—although too often it has been.

***

Bombing abortion clinics is another matter. There is no room for condoning violence. But whatever our substantive views (save one to be addressed in a moment), many other forms of activity in the controversy over abortion since *Roe* (and now since *Webster*) must be seen as acceptable behavior. There have been many actors, public and private, and their actions have taken many forms. What follows are some examples.

First, as much as those of us who favor choice may regret the attempt of state legislatures to limit *Roe,* none of us ought to think that this legislative activity or the private political action that supported and promoted it was improper.

Second, we should not find politically improper the activity of those who peacefully picket abortion clinics or peacefully try to persuade pregnant women to find an alternative. While we may see them as insensitive, if their actions are peaceful they are permissible.

Third, we may find it very unwise and wrongheaded, but not politically improper, for groups to punish pro-choice public servants or to pressure officials to apply a litmus test to government appointments.

Finally, we may want to vote against a president who calls for a constitutional amendment returning the regulation of abortion to the states or employs rhetoric calculated to undermine *Roe,* but we should not find these actions politically improper.

If you favor restrictive abortion laws, you should feel the same way about the activity of pro-choice advocates, which has intensified and become increasingly successful since *Webster.* You should feel this way (and this is the imbalance between pro-choice and pro-life positions) unless you believe that abortion is murder, that a fetus should be entitled to constitutional protection throughout pregnancy. If this is your position, you cannot be very happy with *Webster* (it is only incrementally better than *Roe*), you must be very unhappy about the state of public morality, and you will almost surely want to spend as much time as you can in changing the values that support American attitudes about fetal life and women's rights.

Finally, what are we to think of demonstrations that have taken place in Washington by thousands of people, sometimes hundreds of thousands, aimed directly at persuading the Supreme Court justices to uphold or overturn *Roe?* Notice that such a demonstration is not an attempt to start a law suit and change the law through "litigating elucidation." This distinguishes it from the civil rights activity we have just discussed. Nor are the demonstrations aimed at Congress. We understand when a march on Washington is aimed at bringing pressure to bear on our legislative branch. But a massive demonstration aimed at the Court? Well yes, of course. We should see this as entirely proper although we may think it is politically unwise. A public demonstration is another form of rich dialogue and one that connects with the nature of constitutional adjudication. It is a perfectly respectable aspect of the ubiquitous and diverse dialogue among Americans. It serves a function in the construction of public morality. It shows an intensity of commitment to certain values that are widely shared, values that are a source of law that the Court must weigh in its effort to determine whether *Roe* was a mistake or, more precisely, how much of a mistake *Roe* was.

There are two, nontrivial risks with this form of dialogue. If approved, political activity aimed at the Court may undermine belief in the law. In the teeth of all that we know about the process of adjudication and the sources of law, some persist in seeing the Supreme Court as an apolitical institution. It is not; and as I have tried to show, this is not a sign that the Court is malfunctioning. Accordingly, to approve of political activity directed at the Court is a risk we should take once we know the truth about law and politics. Mendacity is at least as great a risk, as Lincoln taught us when he talked about fooling the people, and truth is its own virtue. Truth does not of course mean what some critical legal scholars seem to say, namely that there is no difference between law and partisan politics.[9] This is as far from reality as the vision of an apolitical Court. I have tried to mark out the difference and to show how distinctive the Court is when compared to other political institutions. Surely we can accept this limited retreat from orthodoxy without abandoning ourselves to the long night of nihilism.

Second, peaceful protest of any kind can lead to violence. But we have had a history of protests leading to violence. It is never welcome, but we can stand it; fortunately America is a strong nation.

To be sure, there has been some violence surrounding the abortion issue. This is unfortunate; it is also inevitable. The constitutionalization of a woman's qualified right to an abortion was bound to be deeply contested. And that is why abortion is a testing case for the view of adjudication advanced in these pages. According to this view, courts are a special environment for the practice of interpretation, and public values—public morality—are a source of law available to judges when they are called on to interpret the Constitution.

While Supreme Court justices are fallible, there generally is acquiescence, if not approval, of their regulatory decisions. This means that even when the Court's constitutional interpretations are seen as a mistake by the majority of Americans, they are easily digested and become law. But sometimes, as with abortion, there is departure from standard practice; then constitutional interpretation by the Court endures only when it is proved by struggle to be politically digestible. Yet what is proved politically digestible turns in part on the Court's prior interpretation. For what the Court decides is both derived from public values and in turn shapes public values. It is this interaction—this complex and robust dialogue—that ultimately makes final the meaning of our fundamental law.

The Constitution of
the United States

We the People of the United States, in Order to form a more perfect Union, establish Justice, insure domestic Tranquility, provide for the common defence, promote the general Welfare, and secure the Blessings of Liberty to ourselves and our Posterity, do ordain and establish this Constitution for the United States of America.

ARTICLE I

SECTION 1. All legislative Powers herein granted shall be vested in a Congress of the United States, which shall consist of a Senate and House of Representatives.

SECTION 2. [1] The House of Representatives shall be composed of Members chosen every second Year by the People of the several States, and the Electors in each State shall have the Qualifications requisite for Electors of the most numerous Branch of the State Legislature.

[2] No Person shall be a Representative who shall not have attained to the Age of twenty five Years, and been seven Years a Citizen of the United States, and who shall not, when elected, be an Inhabitant of that State in which he shall be chosen.

[3] Representatives and direct [Taxes]¹ shall be apportioned among the several States which may be included within this Union, according to their respective Numbers[, which shall be determined by adding to the whole Number of free Persons, including those bound to Service for a Term of

---

1. See Amendment XVI.

Years, and excluding Indians not taxed, three fifths of all other Persons].[2]
The actual Enumeration shall be made within three Years after the first
Meeting of the Congress of the United States, and within every subsequent
Term of ten Years, in such Manner as they shall by Law direct. The Number
of Representatives shall not exceed one for every thirty Thousand, but each
State shall have at Least one Representative; and until such enumeration
shall be made, the State of New Hampshire shall be entitled to chuse three,
Massachusetts eight, Rhode Island and Providence Plantations one, Connecticut five, New York six, New Jersey four, Pennsylvania eight, Delaware
one, Maryland six, Virginia ten, North Carolina five, South Carolina five,
and Georgia three.

[4] When vacancies happen in the Representation from any State, the
Executive Authority thereof shall issue Writs of Election to fill such
Vacancies.

[5] The House of Representatives shall chuse their Speaker and other
Officers; and shall have the sole Power of Impeachment.

SECTION 3. [1] The Senate of the United States shall be composed of two
Senators from each State, [chosen by the Legislature thereof,][3] for six Years;
and each Senator shall have one Vote.

[2] Immediately after they shall be assembled in Consequence of the first
Election, they shall be divided as equally as may be into three Classes. The
Seats of the Senators of the first Class shall be vacated at the Expiration of
the second Year, of the second Class at the Expiration of the fourth Year,
and of the third Class at the Expiration of the sixth Year, so that one third
may be chosen every second Year[; and if Vacancies happen by Resignation,
or otherwise, during the Recess of the Legislature of any State, the Executive
thereof may make temporary Appointments until the next Meeting of the
Legislature, which shall then fill such Vacancies].[4]

[3] No Person shall be a Senator who shall not have attained to the Age
of thirty Years, and been nine Years a Citizen of the United States, and who
shall not, when elected, be an Inhabitant of that State for which he shall be
chosen.

[4] The Vice President of the United States shall be President of the Senate,
but shall have no Vote, unless they be equally divided.

2. See Amendment XIV.
3. See Amendment XVII.
4. See Amendment XVII.

[5] The Senate shall chuse their other Officers, and also a President pro tempore, in the absence of the Vice President, or when he shall exercise the Office of President of the United States.

[6] The Senate shall have the sole Power to try all Impeachments. When sitting for that Purpose, they shall be on Oath or Affirmation. When the President of the United States is tried, the Chief Justice shall preside: And no Person shall be convicted without the Concurrence of two thirds of the Members present.

[7] Judgment in Cases of Impeachment shall not extend further than to removal from Office, and disqualification to hold and enjoy any Office of honor, Trust or Profit under the United States: but the Party convicted shall nevertheless be liable and subject to Indictment, Trial, Judgment and Punishment, according to Law.

SECTION 4. [1] The Times, Places and Manner of holding Elections for Senators and Representatives, shall be prescribed in each State by the Legislature thereof; but the Congress may at any time by Law make or alter such Regulations, except as to the Places of chusing Senators.

[[2] The Congress shall assemble at least once in every Year, and such Meeting shall be on the first Monday in December, unless they shall by Law appoint a different Day.]⁵

SECTION 5. [1] Each House shall be the Judge of the Elections, Returns and Qualifications of its own Members, and a Majority of each shall constitute a Quorum to do Business; but a smaller Number may adjourn from day to day, and may be authorized to compel the Attendance of absent Members, in such Manner, and under such Penalties as each House may provide.

[2] Each House may determine the Rules of its Proceedings, punish its Members for disorderly Behaviour, and, with the Concurrence of two thirds, expel a Member.

[3] Each House shall keep a Journal of its Proceedings, and from time to time publish the same, excepting such Parts as may in their Judgment require Secrecy; and the Yeas and Nays of the Members of either House on any question shall, at the Desire of one fifth of those Present, be entered on the Journal.

[4] Neither House, during the Session of Congress, shall, without the

5. See Amendment XX.

Consent of the other, adjourn for more than three days, nor to any other Place than that in which the two Houses shall be sitting.

SECTION 6. [1] The Senators and Representatives shall receive a Compensation for their Services, to be ascertained by Law, and paid out of the Treasury of the United States. They shall in all Cases, except Treason, Felony and Breach of the Peace, be privileged from Arrest during their Attendance at the Session of their respective Houses, and in going to and returning from the same; and for any Speech or Debate in either House, they shall not be questioned in any other Place.

[2] No Senator or Representative shall, during the Time for which he was elected, be appointed to any civil Office under the Authority of the United States, which shall have been created, or the Emoluments whereof shall have been encreased during such time; and no Person holding any Office under the United States, shall be a Member of either House during his Continuance in Office.

SECTION 7. [1] All Bills for raising Revenue shall originate in the House of Representatives; but the Senate may propose or concur with Amendments as on other Bills.

[2] Every Bill which shall have passed the House of Representatives and the Senate, shall, before it become a Law, be presented to the President of the United States; If he approve he shall sign it, but if not he shall return it, with his Objections to the House in which it shall have originated, who shall enter the Objections at large on their Journal, and proceed to reconsider it. If after such Reconsideration two thirds of that House shall agree to pass the Bill, it shall be sent, together with the Objections, to the other House, by which it shall likewise be reconsidered, and if approved by two thirds of that House, it shall become a Law. But in all such Cases the Votes of both Houses shall be determined by Yeas and Nays, and the Names of the Persons voting for and against the Bill shall be entered on the Journal of each House respectively. If any Bill shall not be returned by the President within ten Days (Sundays excepted) after it shall have been presented to him, the Same shall be a Law, in like Manner as if he had signed it, unless the Congress by their Adjournment prevents its Return, in which Case it shall not be a Law.

[3] Every Order, Resolution, or Vote to which the Concurrence of the Senate and House of Representatives may be necessary (except on a question of Adjournment) shall be presented to the President of the United States; and before the Same shall take Effect, shall be approved by him, or being

disapproved by him, shall be repassed by two thirds of the Senate and House of Representatives, according to the Rules and Limitations prescribed in the Case of a Bill.

SECTION 8. [1] The Congress shall have Power To lay and collect Taxes, Duties, Imposts and Excises, to pay the Debts and provide for the common Defence and general Welfare of the United States; but all Duties, Imposts and Excises shall be uniform throughout the United States;

[2] To borrow money on the credit of the United States;

[3] To regulate Commerce with foreign Nations, and among the several States, and with the Indian Tribes;

[4] To establish an uniform Rule of Naturalization, and uniform Laws on the subject of Bankruptcies throughout the United States;

[5] To coin Money, regulate the Value thereof, and of foreign Coin, and fix the Standard of Weights and Measures;

[6] To provide the Punishment of counterfeiting the Securities and current Coin of the United States;

[7] To establish Post Offices and post Roads;

[8] To promote the Progress of Science and useful Arts, by securing for limited Times to Authors and Inventors the exclusive Right to their respective Writings and Discoveries;

[9] To constitute Tribunals inferior to the supreme Court;

[10] To define and punish Piracies and Felonies committed on the high Seas, and Offenses against the Law of Nations;

[11] To declare War, grant Letters of Marque and Reprisal, and make Rules concerning Captures on Land and Water;

[12] To raise and support Armies, but no Appropriation of Money to that Use shall be for a longer Term than two Years;

[13] To provide and maintain a Navy;

[14] To make Rules for the Government and Regulation of the land and naval Forces;

[15] To provide for calling forth the Militia to execute the Laws of the Union, suppress Insurrections and repel Invasions;

[16] To provide for organizing, arming, and disciplining, the Militia, and for governing such Part of them as may be employed in the Service of the United States, reserving to the States respectively, the Appointment of the Officers, and the Authority of training the Militia according to the discipline prescribed by Congress;

[17] To exercise exclusive Legislation in all Cases whatsoever, over such

District (not exceeding ten Miles square) as may, by Cession of particular States, and the Acceptance of Congress, become the Seat of the Government of the United States, and to exercise like Authority over all Places purchased by the Consent of the Legislature of the State in which the Same shall be, for the Erection of Forts, Magazines, Arsenals, dock-Yards, and other needful Buildings;—And

[18] To make all Laws which shall be necessary and proper for carrying into Execution the foregoing Powers, and all other Powers vested by this Constitution in the Government of the United States, or in any Department or Officer thereof.

SECTION 9. [1] The Migration or Importation of such Persons as any of the States now existing shall think proper to admit, shall not be prohibited by the Congress prior to the Year one thousand eight hundred and eight, but a Tax or duty may be imposed on such Importation, not exceeding ten dollars for each Person.

[2] The privilege of the Writ of Habeas Corpus shall not be suspended, unless when in Cases of Rebellion or Invasion the public Safety may require it.

[3] No Bill of Attainder or ex post facto Law shall be passed.

[[4] No Capitation, or other direct, Tax shall be laid, unless in Proportion to the Census or Enumeration herein before directed to be taken.][6]

[5] No Tax or Duty shall be laid on Articles exported from any State.

[6] No Preference shall be given by any Regulation of Commerce or Revenue to the Ports of one State over those of another; nor shall Vessels bound to, or from, one State, be obliged to enter, clear, or pay Duties in another.

[7] No Money shall be drawn from the Treasury, but in Consequence of Appropriations made by Law; and a regular Statement and Account of the Receipts and Expenditures of all public Money shall be published from time to time.

[8] No Title of Nobility shall be granted by the United States: And no Person holding any Office of Profit or Trust under them, shall, without the Consent of the Congress, accept of any present, Emolument, Office, or Title, of any kind whatever, from any King, Prince, or foreign State.

SECTION 10. [1] No State shall enter into any Treaty, Alliance, or Confederation; grant Letters of Marque and Reprisal; coin Money; emit Bills

6. See Amendment XVI.

of Credit; make any Thing but gold and silver Coin a Tender in Payment of Debts; pass any Bill of Attainder, ex post facto Law, or Law impairing the Obligation of Contracts, or grant any Title of Nobility.

[2] No State shall, without the Consent of the Congress, lay any Imposts or Duties on Imports or Exports, except what may be absolutely necessary for executing its inspection Laws: and the net Produce of all Duties and Imposts, laid by any State on Imports or Exports, shall be for the Use of the Treasury of the United States; and all such Laws shall be subject to the Revision and Controul of the Congress.

[3] No State shall, without the Consent of Congress, lay any Duty of Tonnage, keep Troops, or Ships of War in time of Peace, enter into any Agreement or Compact with another State, or with a foreign Power, or engage in War, unless actually invaded, or in such imminent Danger as will not admit of delay.

ARTICLE II

SECTION 1. [1] The executive Power shall be vested in a President of the United States of America. He shall hold his Office during the Term of four Years, and, together with the Vice President, chosen for the same Term, be elected, as follows:

[2] Each State shall appoint, in such Manner as the Legislature thereof may direct, a Number of Electors, equal to the whole Number of Senators and Representatives to which the State may be entitled in the Congress: but no Senator or Representative, or Person holding an Office of Trust or Profit under the United States, shall be appointed an Elector.

[[3] The Electors shall meet in their respective States, and vote by Ballot for two Persons, of whom one at least shall not be an Inhabitant of the same State with themselves. And they shall make a List of all the Persons voted for, and of the Number of Votes for each; which List they shall sign and certify, and transmit sealed to the Seat of the Government of the United States, directed to the President of the Senate. The President of the Senate shall, in the Presence of the Senate and House of Representatives, open all the Certificates, and the Votes shall then be counted. The Person having the greatest Number of Votes shall be the President, if such Number be a Majority of the whole Number of Electors appointed; and if there be more than one who have such Majority, and have an equal Number of Votes, then the House of Representatives shall immediately chuse by Ballot one of them for President; and if no Person have a Majority, then from the five highest on the List the said House shall in like Manner chuse the President. But in chusing the President, the Votes shall be taken by States, the Representation from each State having one Vote; a quorum for this Purpose shall consist of a Member or Members from two thirds of the States, and a Majority of all the States shall be necessary to a Choice. In every Case, after the Choice of the President, the Person having the greatest Number of Votes of the Electors shall be the Vice President. But if there should remain two or more who have equal Votes, the Senate shall chuse from them by Ballot the Vice President.][7]

[4] The Congress may determine the Time of chusing the Electors, and the Day on which they shall give their Votes; which Day shall be the same throughout the United States.

[5] No person except a natural born Citizen, or a Citizen of the United States, at the time of the Adoption of this Constitution, shall be eligible to the Office of President; neither shall any Person be eligible to that Office who shall not have attained to the Age of thirty five Years, and been fourteen years a Resident within the United States.

[[6] In Case of the removal of the President from Office, or of his Death, Resignation, or Inability to discharge the Powers and Duties of the said Office, the Same shall devolve on the Vice President, and the Congress may by law provide for the Case of Removal, Death, Resignation or Inability, both of the President and Vice President, declaring what Officer shall then act as President, and such Officer shall act accordingly, until the Disability be removed, or a President shall be elected.][8]

[7] The President shall, at stated Times, receive for his Services, a Compensation, which shall neither be increased nor diminished during the Period for which he shall have been elected, and he shall not receive within that Period any other Emolument from the United States, or any of them.

[8] Before he enter on the Execution of his Office, he shall take the following oath or Affirmation: "I do solemnly swear (or affirm) that I will faithfully execute the Office of President of the United States, and will to the best of my Ability, preserve, protect and defend the Constitution of the United States."

---

7. See Amendment XII.
8. See Amendment XXV.

SECTION 2. [1] The President shall be Commander in Chief of the Army and Navy of the United States, and of the Militia of the several States, when called into the actual Service of the United States; he may require the Opinion, in writing, of the principal Officer in each of the executive Departments, upon any Subject relating to the Duties of their respective Offices, and he shall have Power to grant Reprieves and Pardons for Offenses against the United States, except in Cases of Impeachment.

[2] He shall have Power, by and with the Advice and Consent of the Senate, to make Treaties, provided two thirds of the Senators present concur; and he shall nominate, and by and with the Advice and Consent of the Senate, shall appoint Ambassadors, other public Ministers and Consuls, Judges of the supreme Court, and all other Officers of the United States, whose Appointments are not herein otherwise provided for, and which shall be established by Law: but the Congress may by Law vest the Appointment of such inferior Officers, as they think proper, in the President alone, in the Courts of Law, or in the Heads of Departments.

[3] The President shall have Power to fill up all Vacancies that may happen during the Recess of the Senate, by granting Commissions which shall expire at the End of their next Session.

SECTION 3. He shall from time to time give to the Congress Information of the State of the Union, and recommend to their Consideration such Measures as he shall judge necessary and expedient; he may, on extraordinary Occasions, convene both Houses, or either of them, and in Case of Disagreement between them, with Respect to the Time of Adjournment, he may adjourn them to such Time as he shall think proper; he shall receive Ambassadors and other public Ministers; he shall take Care that the Laws be faithfully executed, and shall Commission all the Officers of the United States.

SECTION 4. The President, Vice President and all civil Officers of the United States, shall be removed from Office on Impeachment for, and Conviction of, Treason, Bribery, or other high Crimes and Misdemeanors.

ARTICLE III

SECTION 1. The judicial Power of the United States, shall be vested in one supreme Court, and in such inferior Courts as the Congress may from time to time ordain and establish. The Judges, both of the supreme and inferior

Courts, shall hold their Offices during good Behaviour, and shall, at stated Times, receive for their Services, a Compensation, which shall not be diminished during their Continuance in Office.

SECTION 2. [1] The Judicial Power shall extend to all Cases, in Law and Equity, arising under this Constitution, the Laws of the United States, and Treaties made, or which shall be made, under their Authority;—to all Cases affecting Ambassadors, other public Ministers and Consuls;—to all Cases of admiralty and maritime Jurisdiction;—to Controversies to which the United States shall be a Party;—to Controversies between two or more States;[—between a State and Citizens of another State;]⁹—between Citizens of different States;—between Citizens of the same State claiming Lands under Grants of different States[, and between a State, or the Citizens thereof, and foreign States, Citizens or Subjects].¹⁰

[2] In all Cases affecting Ambassadors, other public Ministers and Consuls, and those in which a State shall be a Party, the supreme Court shall have original Jurisdiction. In all the other Cases before mentioned, the supreme Court shall have appellate Jurisdiction, both as to Law and Fact, with such Exceptions, and under such Regulations as the Congress shall make.

[3] The trial of all Crimes, except in Cases of Impeachment, shall be by Jury; and such Trial shall be held in the State where the said Crimes shall have been committed; but when not committed within any State, the Trial shall be at such Place or Places as the Congress may by Law have directed.

SECTION 3. [1] Treason against the United States, shall consist only in levying War against them, or in adhering to their Enemies, giving them Aid and Comfort. No Person shall be convicted of Treason unless on the Testimony of two Witnesses to the same overt Act, or on Confession in open Court.

[2] The Congress shall have Power to declare the Punishment of Treason, but no Attainder of Treason shall work Corruption of Blood, or Forfeiture except during the Life of the Person attainted.

9. See Amendment XI.
10. See Amendment XI.

ARTICLE IV

SECTION 1. Full Faith and Credit shall be given in each State to the public Acts, Records, and judicial Proceedings of every other State. And the Congress may by general Laws prescribe the Manner in which such Acts, Records and Proceedings shall be proved, and the Effect thereof.

SECTION 2. [1] The Citizens of each State shall be entitled to all Privileges and Immunities of Citizens in the several States.

[2] A Person charged in any State with Treason, Felony, or other Crime, who shall flee from Justice, and be found in another State, shall on demand of the executive Authority of the State from which he fled, be delivered up, to be removed to the State having Jurisdiction of the Crime.

[[3] No Person held to Service or Labour in one State, under the Laws thereof, escaping into another, shall, in Consequence of any Law or Regulation therein, be discharged from such Service or Labour, but shall be delivered up on Claim of the Party to whom such Service or Labour may be due.][11]

SECTION 3. [1] New States may be admitted by the Congress into this Union; but no new State shall be formed or erected within the Jurisdiction of any other State; nor any State be formed by the Junction of two or more States, or Parts of States, without the Consent of the Legislatures of the States concerned as well as of the Congress.

[2] The Congress shall have Power to dispose of and make all needful Rules and Regulations respecting the Territory or other Property belonging to the United States; and nothing in this Constitution shall be so construed as to Prejudice any Claims of the United States, or of any particular State.

SECTION 4. The United States shall guarantee to every State in this Union a Republican Form of Government, and shall protect each of them against Invasion; and on Application of the Legislature, or of the Executive (when the Legislature cannot be convened) against domestic Violence.

ARTICLE V

The Congress, whenever two thirds of both Houses shall deem it necessary, shall propose Amendments to this Constitution, or, on the Application of

11. See Amendment XIII.

the Legislatures of two thirds of the several States, shall call a Convention for proposing Amendments, which, in either Case, shall be valid to all Intents and Purposes, as part of this Constitution, when ratified by the Legislatures of three fourths of the several States, or by Conventions in three fourths thereof, as the one or the other Mode of Ratification may be proposed by the Congress; Provided that no Amendment which may be made prior to the Year One thousand eight hundred and eight shall in any Manner affect the first and fourth Clauses in the Ninth Section of the first Article; and that no State, without its Consent, shall be deprived of its equal Suffrage in the Senate.

ARTICLE VI

[1] All Debts contracted and Engagements entered into, before the Adoption of this Constitution, shall be as valid against the United States under this Constitution, as under the Confederation.

[2] This Constitution, and the Laws of the United States which shall be made in Pursuance thereof; and all Treaties made, or which shall be made, under the Authority of the United States, shall be the supreme Law of the Land; and the Judges in every State shall be bound thereby, any Thing in the Constitution or Laws of any State to the Contrary notwithstanding.

[3] The Senators and Representatives before mentioned, and the Members of the several State Legislatures, and all executive and judicial Officers, both of the United States and of the several States, shall be bound by Oath or Affirmation, to support this Constitution; but no religious Test shall ever be required as a Qualification to any Office or public Trust under the United States.

ARTICLE VII

The Ratification of the Conventions of nine States shall be sufficient for the Establishment of this Constitution between the States so ratifying the Same.

Done in Convention by the Unanimous Consent of the States present the Seventeenth Day of September in the Year of our Lord one thousand seven hundred and Eighty seven and of the Independence of the United States of America the Twelfth.

ARTICLES IN ADDITION TO, AND AMENDMENT OF, THE CONSTITUTION OF THE UNITED STATES OF AMERICA, PROPOSED BY CONGRESS, AND RATIFIED BY THE LEGISLATURES OF THE SEVERAL STATES, PURSUANT TO THE FIFTH ARTICLE OF THE ORIGINAL CONSTITUTION

AMENDMENT I [1791]

Congress shall make no law respecting an establishment of religion, or prohibiting the free exercise thereof; or abridging the freedom of speech, or of the press; or the right of the people peaceably to assemble, and to petition the Government for a redress of grievances.

AMENDMENT II [1791]

A well regulated Militia, being necessary to the security of a free State, the right of the people to keep and bear Arms, shall not be infringed.

AMENDMENT III [1791]

No Soldier shall, in time of peace be quartered in any house, without the consent of the Owner, nor in time of war, but in a manner to be prescribed by law.

AMENDMENT IV [1791]

The right of the people to be secure in their persons, houses, papers, and effects, against unreasonable searches and seizures, shall not be violated, and no Warrants shall issue, but upon probable cause, supported by Oath or affirmation, and particularly describing the place to be searched, and the persons or things to be seized.

AMENDMENT V [1791]

No person shall be held to answer for a capital, or otherwise infamous crime, unless on a presentment or indictment of a Grand Jury, except in cases arising in the land or naval forces, or in the Militia, when in actual service in time of War or public danger; nor shall any person be subject for the same offence to be twice put in jeopardy of life or limb; nor shall be compelled in any criminal case to be a witness against himself, nor be deprived of life, liberty, or property, without due process of law; nor shall private property be taken for public use, without just compensation.

AMENDMENT VI [1791]

In all criminal prosecutions, the accused shall enjoy the right to a speedy and public trial, by an impartial jury of the State and district wherein the crime shall have been committed, which district shall have been previously ascertained by law, and to be informed of the nature and cause of the accusation; to be confronted with the witnesses against him; to have compulsory process for obtaining witnesses in his favor, and to have the Assistance of Counsel for his defence.

AMENDMENT VII [1791]

In Suits at common law, where the value in controversy shall exceed twenty dollars, the right of trial by jury shall be preserved, and no fact tried by a jury, shall be otherwise re-examined in any Court of the United States, than according to the rules of the common law.

AMENDMENT VIII [1791]

Excessive bail shall not be required, nor excessive fines imposed, nor cruel and unusual punishments inflicted.

AMENDMENT IX [1791]

The enumeration in the Constitution, of certain rights, shall not be construed to deny or disparage others retained by the people.

AMENDMENT X [1791]

The powers not delegated to the United States by the Constitution, nor prohibited by it to the States, are reserved to the States respectively, or to the people.

AMENDMENT XI [1798]

The Judicial power of the United States shall not be construed to extend to any suit in law or equity, commenced or prosecuted against one of the United States by Citizens of another State, or by Citizens or Subjects of any Foreign State.

AMENDMENT XII [1804]

The Electors shall meet in their respective states and vote by ballot for President and Vice-President, one of whom, at least, shall not be an inhabitant of the same state with themselves; they shall name in their ballots the person voted for as President, and in distinct ballots the person voted for as Vice-President, and they shall make distinct lists of all persons voted for as President, and of all persons voted for as Vice-President, and of the number of votes for each, which lists they shall sign and certify, and transmit sealed to the seat of the government of the United States, directed to the President of the Senate;—The President of the Senate shall, in the presence of the Senate and House of Representatives, open all the certificates and the votes shall then be counted;—The person having the greatest number of votes for President, shall be the President, if such number be a majority of the whole number of Electors appointed; and if no person have such majority, then from the persons having the highest numbers not exceeding three on the list of those voted for as President, the House of Representatives shall choose immediately, by ballot, the President. But in choosing the President, the votes shall be taken by states, the representation from each state having one vote; a quorum for this purpose shall consist of a member or members from two-thirds of the states, and a majority of all the states shall be necessary to a choice. And if the House of Representatives shall not choose a President whenever the right of choice shall devolve upon them, before the fourth day of March next following, then the Vice-President shall act as President, as in the case of the death or other constitutional disability of the President.—The person having the greatest number of votes as Vice-President, shall be the Vice-President, if such number be a majority of the whole number of Electors appointed, and if no person have a majority, then from the two highest numbers on the list, the Senate shall choose the Vice-President; a quorum for the purpose shall consist of two-thirds of the whole number of Senators, and a majority of the whole number shall be necessary to a choice. But no person constitutionally ineligible to the office of President shall be eligible to that of Vice-President of the United States.

AMENDMENT XIII [1865]

SECTION 1. Neither slavery nor involuntary servitude, except as a punishment for crime whereof the party shall have been duly convicted, shall exist within the United States, or any place subject to their jurisdiction.

SECTION 2. Congress shall have power to enforce this article by appropriate legislation.

AMENDMENT XIV [1868]

SECTION 1. All persons born or naturalized in the United States, and subject to the jurisdiction thereof, are citizens of the United States and of the State wherein they reside. No State shall make or enforce any law which shall abridge the privileges or immunities of citizens of the United States; nor shall any State deprive any person of life, liberty, or property, without due process of law; nor deny to any person within its jurisdiction the equal protection of the laws.

SECTION 2. Representatives shall be apportioned among the several States according to their respective numbers, counting the whole number of persons in each State, excluding Indians not taxed. But when the right to vote at any election for the choice of electors for President and Vice President of the United States, Representatives in Congress, the Executive and Judicial officers of a State, or the members of the Legislature thereof, is denied to any of the male inhabitants of such State, being twenty-one years of age, and citizens of the United States, or in any way abridged, except for participation in rebellion, or other crime, the basis of representation therein shall be reduced in the proportion which the number of such male citizens shall bear to the whole number of male citizens twenty-one years of age in such State.

SECTION 3. No person shall be a Senator or Representative in Congress, or elector of President and Vice President, or hold any office, civil or military, under the United States, or under any State, who, having previously taken an oath, as a member of Congress, or as an officer of the United States, or as a member of any State legislature, or as an executive or judicial officer of any State, to support the Constitution of the United States, shall have engaged in insurrection or rebellion against the same, or given aid or comfort to the enemies thereof. But Congress may by a vote of two-thirds of each House, remove such disability.

SECTION 4. The validity of the public debt of the United States, authorized by law, including debts incurred for payment of pensions and bounties for services in suppressing insurrection or rebellion, shall not be questioned. But neither the United States nor any State shall assume or pay any debt or obligation incurred in aid of insurrection or rebellion against the United States, or any claim for the loss of emancipation of any slave; but all such debts, obligations and claims shall be held illegal and void.

SECTION 5. The Congress shall have power to enforce, by appropriate legislation, the provisions of this article.

AMENDMENT XV [1870]

SECTION 1. The right of citizens of the United States to vote shall not be denied or abridged by the United States or by any State on account of race, color, or previous condition of servitude.

SECTION 2. The Congress shall have power to enforce this article by appropriate legislation.

AMENDMENT XVI [1913]

The Congress shall have power to lay and collect taxes on incomes, from whatever source derived, without apportionment among the several States, and without regard to any census or enumeration.

AMENDMENT XVII [1913]

[1] The Senate of the United States shall be composed of two Senators from each State, elected by the people thereof, for six years; and each Senator shall have one vote. The electors in each State shall have the qualifications requisite for electors of the most numerous branch of the State legislatures.

[2] When vacancies happen in the representation of any State in the Senate, the executive authority of such State shall issue writs of election to fill such vacancies: *Provided,* That the legislature of any State may empower the executive thereof to make temporary appointments until the people fill the vacancies by election as the legislature may direct.

[3] This amendment shall not be. so construed as to affect the election or term of any Senator chosen before it becomes valid as part of the Constitution.

AMENDMENT XVIII [1919]

SECTION 1. After one year from the ratification of this article the manufacture, sale, or transportation of intoxicating liquors within, the importation thereof into, or the exportation thereof from the United States and all territory subject to the jurisdiction thereof for beverage purposes is hereby prohibited.

SECTION 2. The Congress and the several States shall have concurrent power to enforce this article by appropriate legislation.

SECTION 3. This article shall be inoperative unless it shall have been ratified as an amendment to the Constitution by the legislatures of the several States, as provided in the Constitution, within seven years from the date of the submission hereof to the States by the Congress.[12]

12. See Amendment XXI.

AMENDMENT XIX [1920]

[1] The right of citizens of the United States to vote shall not be denied or abridged by the United States or by any State on account of sex.

[2] Congress shall have power to enforce this article by appropriate legislation.

AMENDMENT XX [1933]

SECTION 1. The terms of the President and Vice President shall end at noon on the 20th day of January, and the terms of Senators and Representatives at noon on the 3d day of January, of the years in which such terms would have ended if this article had not been ratified; and the terms of their successors shall then begin.

SECTION 2. The Congress shall assemble at least once in every year, and such meeting shall begin at noon on the 3d of January, unless they shall by law appoint a different day.

SECTION 3. If, at the time fixed for the beginning of the term of the President, the President elect shall have died, the Vice President elect shall become President. If a President shall not have been chosen before the time fixed for the beginning of his term, or if the President elect shall have failed to qualify, then the Vice President elect shall act as President until a President shall have qualified; and the Congress may by law provide for the case wherein neither a President elect nor a Vice President elect shall have qualified, declaring who shall then act as President, or the manner in which one who is to act shall be selected, and such person shall act accordingly until a President or Vice President shall have qualified.

SECTION 4. The Congress may by law provide for the case of the death of any of the persons from whom the House of Representatives may choose a President whenever the right of choice shall have devolved upon them, and for the case of the death of any of the persons from whom the Senate may choose a Vice President whenever the right of choice shall have devolved upon them.

SECTION 5. Sections 1 and 2 shall take effect on the 15th day of October following the ratification of this article.

SECTION 6. This article shall be inoperative unless it shall have been ratified as an amendment to the Constitution by the legislatures of three-fourths of the several States within seven years from the date of its submission.

AMENDMENT XXI [1933]

SECTION 1. The eighteenth article of amendment to the Constitution of the United States is hereby repealed.

SECTION 2. The transportation or importation into any State, Territory, or possession of the United States for delivery or use therein of intoxicating liquors, in violation of the laws thereof, is hereby prohibited.

SECTION 3. This article shall be inoperative unless it shall have been ratified as an amendment to the Constitution by conventions in the several States, as provided in the Constitution, within seven years from the date of the submission hereof to the States by the Congress.

AMENDMENT XXII [1951]

SECTION 1. No person shall be elected to the office of the President more than twice, and no person who has held the office of President, or acted as President, for more than two years of a term to which some other person was elected President shall be elected to the office of the President more than once. But this Article shall not apply to any person holding the office of President when this Article was proposed by the Congress, and shall not prevent any person who may be holding the office of President, or acting as President, during the term within which the Article becomes operative from holding the office of President or acting as President during the remainder of such term.

SECTION 2. This article shall be inoperative unless it shall have been ratified as an amendment to the Constitution by the legislatures of three-fourths of the several States within seven years from the date of its submission to the States by the Congress.

AMENDMENT XXIII [1961]

SECTION 1. The District constituting the seat of Government of the United States shall appoint in such manner as the Congress may direct:

A number of electors of President and Vice President equal to the whole number of Senators and Representatives in Congress to which the District would be entitled if it were a State, but in no event more than the least populous State; they shall be in addition to those appointed by the States, but they shall be considered, for the purposes of the election of President and Vice President, to be electors appointed by a State; and they shall meet in the District and perform such duties as provided by the twelfth article of amendment.

SECTION 2. The Congress shall have power to enforce this article by appropriate legislation.

AMENDMENT XXIV [1964]

SECTION 1. The right of citizens of the United States to vote in any primary or other election for President or Vice President, for electors for President or Vice President, or for Senator or Representative in Congress, shall not be denied or abridged by the United States or any State by reason of failure to pay any poll tax or other tax.

SECTION 2. The Congress shall have power to enforce this article by appropriate legislation.

AMENDMENT XXV [1967]

SECTION 1. In case of the removal of the President from office or of his death or resignation, the Vice President shall become President.

SECTION 2. Whenever there is a vacancy in the office of the Vice President, the President shall nominate a Vice President who shall take office upon confirmation by a majority vote of both Houses of Congress.

SECTION 3. Whenever the President transmits to the President pro tempore of the Senate and the Speaker of the House of Representatives his written declaration that he is unable to discharge the powers and duties of his office, and until he transmits to them a written declaration to the contrary, such powers and duties shall be discharged by the Vice President as Acting President.

SECTION 4. Whenever the Vice President and a majority of either the principal officers of the executive departments or of such other body as

Congress may by law provide, transmit to the President pro tempore of the Senate and the Speaker of the House of Representatives their written declaration that the President is unable to discharge the powers and duties of his office, the Vice President shall immediately assume the powers and duties of the office as Acting President.

Thereafter, when the President transmits to the President pro tempore of the Senate and the Speaker of the House of Representatives his written declaration that no inability exists, he shall resume the powers and duties of his office unless the Vice President and a majority of either the principal officers of the executive department or of such other body as Congress may by law provide, transmit within four days to the President pro tempore of the Senate and the Speaker of the House of Representatives their written declaration that the President is unable to discharge the powers and duties of his office. Thereupon Congress shall decide the issue, assembling within forty-eight hours for that purpose if not in session. If the Congress, within twenty-one days after receipt of the latter written declaration, or, if Congress is not in session, within twenty-one days after Congress is required to assemble, determines by two-thirds vote of both Houses that the President is unable to discharge the powers and duties of his office, the Vice President shall continue to discharge the same as Acting President; otherwise, the President shall resume the powers and duties of his office.

AMENDMENT XXVI [1971]

SECTION 1. The right of citizens of the United States, who are eighteen years of age or older, to vote shall not be denied or abridged by the United States or by any State on account of age.

SECTION 2. The Congress shall have power to enforce this article by appropriate legislation.

NOTES

CHAPTER 1 *Regulation and Dispute Resolution*

1. *Goldman v. Weinberger*, 475 U.S. 503 (1986).

2. "[A] member of the armed forces may wear an item of religious apparel while wearing the uniform of the member's armed force [except] (1) [where] the Secretary determines that the wearing of the item would interfere with the performance of the member's military duties; or (2) . . . that item of apparel is not neat and conservative." 10 U.S.C.A. §774 (1989).

3. *Roe v. Wade*, 410 U.S. 113 (1973). Efforts have been made in Congress (but no statute has been passed) to overturn *Roe* by legislation based on section 5 of the Fourteenth Amendment. Such legislation would almost surely be unconstitutional.

4. *Webster v. Reproductive Health Services*, 109 S. Ct. 3040 (1989).

5. An interesting view of the duty that courts should assume because of this legislative work load, among other factors, may be found in G. Calabresi, *A Common Law for the Age of Statutes* (Cambridge: Harvard University Press, 1982).

6. See S. Fish, *Is There a Text in This Class? The Authority of Interpretive Communities* (Cambridge: Harvard University Press, 1980).

7. R. Dworkin, *A Matter of Principle* (Cambridge: Harvard University Press, 1985), 119–45.

8. John Milton, *Areopagitica* (1644).

9. B. Woodward and S. Armstrong, *The Brethren* (New York: Simon and Schuster, 1979), is an example of investigative reporting. D. O'Brien, *Storm Center: The Supreme Court in American Politics* (New York: W. W. Norton, 1986), and B. Schwartz with S. Lesher, *Inside the Warren Court* (Garden City, N.Y.: Doubleday, 1983), are examples of scholarship.

10. *Bradwell v. State of Illinois*, 16 Wall 130, 141 (1873).

11. *Goesaert v. Cleary,* 335 U.S. 464 (1948).

12. *Craig v. Boren,* 429 U.S. 190, 197 (1976).

CHAPTER 2 *Judicial Review*

1. *Marbury v. Madison,* 1 Cranch 137 (1803).

2. *The Federalist* No. 78, at 466 (A. Hamilton) (C. Rossiter ed. 1961).

3. C. Black, *The People and the Court: Judicial Review in a Democracy* (New York: Macmillan, 1960; repr. 1977). The first quotation is at p. 52, the second at p. 53.

4. A. Bickel, *The Least Dangerous Branch* (Indianapolis and New York: Bobbs-Merrill, 1962; repr. 1986). The quotation is at p. 3. The next long quotation is at p. 24.

5. Bickel, *Least Dangerous Branch,* 18.

6. K. Arrow, *Social Choice and Individual Values,* 2d ed. (New York: John Wiley and Sons, 1963). For a good explanation of this literature see Farber and Frickey, "The Jurisprudence of Public Choice," 65 *Tex L. Rev.* 873 (1987).

7. *Buckley v. Valeo,* 424 U.S. 1 (1976).

8. "In 1986, 98 percent of the [House] incumbents won [reelection]." *New York Times,* September 25, 1988, sec. 4, p. 1.

9. On these matters the literature is extensive. I have found the following books most helpful: R. Arnold, *Congress and the Bureaucracy: A Theory of Influence* (New Haven and London: Yale University Press, 1979); J. Choper, *Judicial Review and the National Political Process: A Functional Reconsideration of the Role of the Supreme Court* (Chicago: University of Chicago Press, 1980); R. Fenno, *Congressmen in Committee* (Boston: Little, Brown, 1973); M. Fiorina, *Congress, Keystone of the Washington Establishment* (New Haven and London: Yale University Press, 1977); M. Malbin, *Unelected Representatives: Congressional Staff and the Future of Representative Government* (New York: Basic Books, 1980); K. Schlozman and J. Tierney, *Organized Interests and American Democracy* (New York: Harper and Row, 1986).

10. Stigler, "The Theory of Economic Regulation," 2 *Bell J. Econ & Mgmt. Sci.* 3, 11 (1971).

11. *NLRB v. Virginia Electric & Power Co.,* 314 U.S. 469 (1941).

12. One such lapse is *International Longshoremen's Ass'n v. Allied International Inc.,* 456 U.S. 212 (1982). The case held that the First Amendment did not protect the peaceful picketing of ships destined for the Soviet Union by union members protesting the Soviet invasion of Afghanistan.

13. *Edward J. DeBartolo Corp. v. Florida Gulf Coast Bldg. & Constr. Trades Council,* 485 U.S. 568 (1988).

14. *Textile Workers Union v. Darlington Manufacturing Co.,* 380 U.S. 263 (1965).

15. See for example *Ferguson v. Skrupa,* 372 U.S. 726 (1963).

16. *Steele v. Louisville & N.R.R.,* 323 U.S. 192, 202 (1944).

17. Bickel, *Least Dangerous Branch,* 111–98.

18. *Fullilove v. Klutznick,* 448 U.S. 448, 549–50 (1980).

19. *Miranda v. Arizona,* 384 U.S. 436 (1966); *Linkletter v. Walker,* 381 U.S. 616 (1965); *Mapp v. Ohio,* 367 U.S. 643 (1961).

20. R. Dahl, *Democracy and Its Critics* (New Haven and London: Yale University Press, 1989), 188–89.

21. *Railway Express Agency v. New York,* 336 U.S. 106, 112 (1949).

CHAPTER 3 *Original Intent*

1. Wechsler, "Toward Neutral Principles of Constitutional Law," 73 *Harv. L. Rev.* 1, 15 (1959).

2. *Brown v. Board of Education,* 347 U.S. 483 (1954).

3. See generally Tushnet, "Following the Rules Laid Down: A Critique of Interpretivism and Neutral Principles," 96 *Harv. L. Rev.* 781 (1983).

4. Bork, "Neutral Principles and Some First Amendment Problems," 47 *Ind. L.J.* 21 (1971).

5. *Griswold v. Connecticut,* 381 U.S. 479 (1965).

6. *Eisenstadt v. Baird,* 405 U.S. 438 (1972), is the contraception case. *Roe v. Wade,* 410 U.S. 113 (1973), is the abortion decision.

7. *Lochner v. New York,* 198 U.S. 45 (1905).

8. *Nebbia v. New York,* 291 U.S. 502 (1934); *West Coast Hotel Co. v. Parrish,* 300 U.S. 379 (1937).

9. *Roe v. Wade,* 410 U.S. 113 (1973).

10. See Brest, "The Misconceived Quest for Original Understanding," 60 *B.U. L. Rev.* 204 (1980).

11. These remarks were made on May 8, 1987, at the judicial conference of the Court of Appeals for the Federal Circuit. See 119 F.R.D. 45, 68 (1988).

12. L. Levy, "Constitutional History, 1776–1789," *American Constitutional History* (New York: Macmillan, 1989), ed. L. Levy et al., 18–36.

13. Powell, "The Original Understanding of Original Intent," 98 *Harv. L. Rev.* 885, 948 (1985).

14. Hutson, "The Creation of the Constitution: The Integrity of the Documentary Record," 65 *Tex. L. Rev.* 1, 2 (1986).

15. E. Morgan, *The Birth of the Republic, 1763–89* (Chicago: University of Chicago Press, 1956), 16.

16. *Republic Aviation Corp. v. NLRB*, 324 U.S. 793 (1945).

17. "On July 26 [1787] the [Constitutional] Convention adjourned until August 6 to allow a Committee on Detail to frame a 'constitution conformable to the Resolutions passed by the Convention.' Generously construing its charge, the committee acted as a miniature convention and introduced a number of significant changes." Levy, "Constitutional History," 32.

18. "Justice Black and First Amendment 'Absolutes': A Public Interview, 37 *N.Y.U. L. Rev.* 549, 553 (1962) (footnotes omitted).

19. Black, "The Bill of Rights," 35 *N.Y.U. L. Rev.* 865, 867 (1960).

20. See L. Levy, *Legacy of Suppression: Freedom of Speech and Press in Early American History* (Cambridge: Harvard University Press/Belknap, 1960), vii.

21. Bork, "Neutral Principles and Some First Amendment Problems," 47 *Ind. L.J.* 1, 21 (1971).

22. "Justice Black and the First Amendment 'Absolutes,' " 553.

23. See *Adamson v. California*, 332 U.S. 46, 68 (Black, J., dissenting).

24. See for example *Duncan v. Louisiana*, 391 U.S. 145, 162 (1968) (Black, J., concurring).

CHAPTER 4 *Policing Participation*

1. *Lochner v. New York*, 198 U.S. 45 (1905).

2. *Lochner v. New York*, 69–70.

3. *Lochner v. New York*, 75.

4. See for example *Carter v. Carter Coal Co.*, 298 U.S. 238 (1936).

5. See for example *Nebbia v. New York,* 291 U.S. 502 (1934); *West Coast Hotel Co. v. Parrish,* 300 U.S. 379 (1937).

6. *United States v. Carolene Products Co.,* 304 U.S. 144 (1938).

7. *United States v. Carolene Products Co.,* 152n.

8. The phrase is John Hart Ely's. See J. Ely, *Democracy and Distrust: A Theory of Judicial Review* (Cambridge: Harvard University Press, 1980), 87.

9. Ackerman, "Beyond Carolene Products," 98 *Harv. L. Rev.* 713 (1985).

10. Ely, *Democracy and Distrust,* 103 (emphasis in original, footnote omitted).

11. See *Reynolds v. Sims,* 377 U.S. 533 (1964).

12. Ely, *Democracy and Distrust,* 106.

13. *New York Times v. Sullivan,* 376 U.S. 254 (1964). See for example *Gertz v. Robert Welch, Inc.,* 418 U.S. 323 (1974).

14. Ely, *Democracy and Distrust,* 75n.

15. See generally Wertheimer, "Campaign Finance Reform," *Annals of the American Academy,* no. 486 (July 1986): 86.

16. Thayer, "The Origin and Scope of the American Doctrine of Constitutional Law," 7 *Harv. L. Rev.* 129 (1893).

CHAPTER 5 *Sources of Law*

1. A. Bickel, *The Least Dangerous Branch* (Indianapolis and New York: Bobbs-Merrill, 1962; repr. 1986), 24.

2. Compare Fiss, "Objectivity and Interpretation," 34 *Stan. L. Rev.* 739 (1982); Fiss, "Conventionalism," 58 *S. Cal. L. Rev.* 177 (1985).

3. See for example D. O'Brien, *Storm Center: The Supreme Court in American Politics* (New York: W. W. Norton, 1986), 213–75.

4. Bickel, *Least Dangerous Branch,* 24.

5. *Craig v. Boren,* 429 U.S. 190, 197 (1976).

6. J. Ely, *Democracy and Distrust: A Theory of Judicial Review* (Cambridge: Harvard University Press, 1980).

7. *Texas v. Johnson,* 109 S. Ct. 2533 (1989). The statute mentioned in the next paragraph is the Flag Protection Act of 1989, 18 U.S.C.A. §700 (Supp. 1990). The Court declared it unconstitutional in *United States v. Eichman,* 58 L.W. 4744 (1990).

8. *Griswold v. Connecticut,* 381 U.S. 479, 480 (1965).

9. *Poe v. Ullman,* 367 U.S. 497, 546 (1961) (Harlan, J., dissenting). *Poe v. Ullman* was an earlier case involving the Connecticut statute, but the Court did not there reach the constitutional question. Harlan, in dissent, wrote that the statute violated due process. What he said on the merits in Poe, he incorporated by reference into his opinion in *Griswold.*

10. See generally J. D'Emilio and E. Freedman, *Intimate Matters: A History of Sexuality in America* (New York: Harper and Row, 1988).

11. 381 U.S. at 507.

12. *Meyer v. Nebraska,* 262 U.S. 390, 400 (1923).

13. *Pierce v. Society of Sisters,* 268 U.S. 510, 536 (1925).

CHAPTER 6 *Public Morality*

1. *Roe v. Wade,* 410 U.S. 113 (1973).

2. *Webster v. Reproductive Health Services,* 109 S. Ct. 3040 (1989). *Hodgson v. Minnesota,* 58 L.W. 4957 (1990), and *Ohio v. Akron Center for Reproductive Health,* 58 L.W. 4979 (1990), were decided by the Court on June 25. Both involved the constitutionality of requiring parental notification before an abortion could be performed on a minor. See note 16 to chapter 6, below.

3. Thomson, "A Defense of Abortion," 1 *Phil. & Pub. Affairs* 47, 66 (1971). The next quotation in the text from this article is at Thomson, p. 48.

4. Compare *Jacobsen v. Massachusetts,* 187 U.S. 11 (1905), with *Cruzan v. Director, Missouri Department of Health,* 58 L.W. 4916 (1990).

5. *Doe v. Bolton,* 410 U.S. 179 (1973).

6. For a summary of the diversity of state laws on abortion at the time of *Webster,* see *New York Times, June* 25, 1989, sec. 1, p. 20.

7. *Griffin v. Illinois,* 351 U.S. 12 (1956).

8. See for example *San Antonio Independent School Dist. v. Rodriguez,* 411 U.S. 1 (1973). In the context of financing public education, the Court held that poor is not a suspect classification and education is not a fundamental right. The case came from Texas. Local property taxes financed education within a school district and there were vast differences in per-pupil expenditures among rich and poor districts within the state.

9. The two principal cases on public funding are *Maher v. Roe,* 432 U.S. 464 (1977) and *Harris v. McRae,* 448 U.S. 297 (1980).

10. See generally *Akron v. Akron Center for Reproductive Health*, 462 U.S. 416 (1983); *Missouri v. Danforth*, 428 (1976) (spousal consent).

11. See *Akron v. Akron Center for Reproductive Health*, 462 U.S. 416 (1983).

12. *Brown v. Board of Education*, 347 U.S. 483 (1954).

13. *Engel v. Vitale*, 370 U.S. 421 (1962); *Abington School Dist. v. Schempp*, 374 U.S. 203 (1963). See *Wallace v. Jaffree*, 472 U.S. 38 (1985).

14. See *Akron v. Akron Center for Reproductive Health*, 462 U.S. 416, 460–61 (1983) (emphasis in original).

15. What Justice White actually said was that "the State's interest, if compelling after viability, is equally compelling before viability." *Thornburgh v. American Coll. of Obst. & Gyn.*, 476 U.S. 747, 795 (1986) (footnote omitted).

Justice O'Connor said this: "The State has compelling interests in ensuring maternal health and in protecting potential human life, and the interests exist 'throughout pregnancy.' " *Thornburgh v. American Coll. of Obst. & Gyn.*, 476 U.S. 747, 828 (1986).

16. *Thornburgh v. American Coll. of Obst. & Gyn.*, 476 U.S. 747, 828 (1986). In *Hodgson v. Minnesota*, 58 L.W. 4957, 4968 (1990), Justice O'Connor agreed with the Court about the unconstitutionality of a state law requiring notification of both parents before an abortion could be performed on a woman under eighteen.

17. *Thornburgh v. American Coll. of Obst. & Gyn.*, 476 U.S. 747, 785–814 (1986).

18. The plurality opinion in *Webster* (joined by Justice White) seems to acknowledge that "23½ to 24 weeks gestation is the earliest point in pregnancy where a reasonable possibility of viability exists." *Webster v. Reproductive Health Services*, 109 Sup. Ct. 3040, 3055 (1989) (quoting the finding of the District Court).

19. *Bowers v. Hardwick*, 478 U.S. 186 (1986).

20. *Carey v. Population Services International*, 431 U.S. 876 (1976).

21. *Stanley v. Georgia*, 394 U.S. 557 (1969), quoted in *Bowers v. Hardwick*, 478 U.S. 186, 195 (1986).

CHAPTER 7 *Judicial Mistake*

1. *Chisholm v. Georgia*, 2 Dall. 419 (1793).

2. *Dred Scott v. Sandford,* 19 How. 393 (1857).

3. *Pollock v. Farmer's Loan and Trust Co.,* 157 U.S. 429 (1895).

4. *Oregon v. Mitchell,* 400 U.S. 112 (1970).

5. See for example Ackerman, "The Storrs Lectures: Discovering the Constitution," 93 *Yale L. J.* 1013 (1984); Ackerman, "Constitutional Politics/Constitutional Law," 99 *Yale L. J.* 453 (1989).

6. *Ex Parte McCardle,* 7 Wall. 506 (1869).

7. Norris-LaGuardia Act, 29 U.S.C. §101–15 (1982).

8. Meese, "The Law of the Constitution," 61 *Tulane L. Rev.* 979, 983 (1987).

9. *Cooper v. Aaron,* 358 U.S. 1, 17–18 (1958).

10. Gunther, "The Subtle Vices of the 'Passive Virtues': A Comment on Principle and Expediency in Judicial Review," 64 *Colum. L. Rev.* 1, 25 (1964).

11. *New York Times v. Sullivan,* 376 U.S. 254 (1964).

12. *Olmstead v. United States,* 277 U.S. 438, 471–85 (1928).

13. B. Cardozo, *The Nature of the Judicial Process* (New Haven: Yale University Press, 1921), 22.

14. See for example Klevorick & Rothschild, "A Model of the Jury Decision Process," 8 *J. Legal Stud.* 141 (1979); Levin, "Education, Life Chances, and the Courts: The Role of Social Science Evidence," 39 *Law & Contemp. Probs.* 217 (1975).

CHAPTER 8 *The Court's Constitutional Interpretation*

1. *National League of Cities v. Usery,* 426 U.S. 833 (1976).

2. *Maryland v. Wirtz,* 392 U.S. 183 (1968).

3. *Garcia v. San Antonio Transit Authority,* 469 U.S. 528 (1985).

4. The letter is dated September 11, 1804. It is reproduced in Gunther, *Constitutional Law,* 11th ed. (Mineola, N.Y.: Foundation Press, 1985), 22.

5. The first paragraph is from a speech delivered on July 10, 1858; the second is from a speech delivered on October 13, 1858. Both speeches are excerpted in Gunther, *Constitutional Law,* 23.

6. *McCulloch v. Maryland,* 4 Wheat. 316 (1819).

7. A. Bickel, *The Least Dangerous Branch* (Indianapolis and New York: Bobbs-Merrill, 1962; repr. 1986), 111–98; Gunther, "The Subtle Vices of

the 'Passive Virtues': A Comment on Principle and Expediency in Judicial Review," 64 *Colum. L. Rev.* 1 (1964).

8. The state action issue, however, was not resolved, as such, in the lunch counter sit-in cases. See for example *Peterson v. Greenville,* 373 U.S. 244 (1963); *Bell v. Maryland,* 378 U.S. 226 (1964).

9. For an interesting account of constitutional theory, written by a critical legal scholar, see M. Tushnet, *Red, White and Blue: A Critical Analysis of Constitutional Law* (Cambridge: Harvard University Press, 1988).